HAGAR'S COMMUNITY CHURCH

Fury and Grace

40 Days of Paintings and Poetry from Prison

To those who wait in prison
For the breaking of a new and glorious morning
To all the lonely and the searching
To mamas missing their babies
Daughters missing their mamas and
Nanas missing their grandbabies
May you discover deep meaning
In your waiting
Alongside our Beloved friend
Sweet Jesus
May your darkness
Be the cradle of the dawn

All Glory to God: the arrested, executed, and resurrected One

Contents

V With Us in the Wilderness

VI   Storytelling with the Holy Spirit

VII The Arrested, Executed and Resurrected One

Preface

What does "fury" mean to you? What does it mean to be furious? Have you ever been furious before? Fury is an emotion; all of our emotions are connected to God or can help us learn more about ourselves and our relationship to God - and that includes fury. We hope this book will not only allow you to perhaps become furious about things such as the injustices of our world - but also will allow you to become delighted, challenged, and curious along the way. Through your fury may you discover God's grace.

This pilgrimage of art and poetry was co-created, weaved together with a diverse array of voices, fed from the wells of the imaginations of many. We invite you to join in and become a co-creator alongside these authors, poets, and artists as we journey together through this book and this season of Lent.

This book follows the Revised Common Daily Lectionary passages for Year B. For every day in Lent and Holy Week, you'll encounter art, reflections, and prayers to guide you along the way. The book is separated by parts which divide the season into seven weeks, each of which has a broad theme. Each chapter of the book represents a day, titled in such a way to help you think of it as a world of its own into which you are entering and through which you are being opened up to all it has to offer. Use this book however works best for you. Read it in the morning with your coffee or tea. Use it as a midday soul-break. Wind down with the pages before you go to sleep. Let it stir you, challenge and comfort, inspire and invigorate.

As you meditate, pray, sing, read, take in, soak up, and engage these offerings, make it your own. Underline, write, color, draw, and respond in the margins. Fold down the corners of pages you want to come back to and write yourself a little love note that you'll find, perhaps even long after you have forgotten that you've written it. This book is inherently a *communal journey* and God, who is closer than our very breath, is with us every step of the way.

-Rev. Riley Pickett & Revs. Layne and Crawford Brubaker

Spiritual Practices to Complement and Supplement This Book

Art and Poetry

This book came about because Hagar's Community Church had to adapt to all the restrictions of worshipping through a pandemic. Responding creatively through art and poetry became our worship—and this book springs forth from that worship. As you journey through this Lenten Devotional we encourage you to also respond creatively each day. Do not worry about it being perfect—don't worry if you have never painted before, or if your elementary art teacher said you were terrible at art, or if you have never written a poem or ... just relax. Allow your spirit to play with crayons, or pencils, or clay, or words, or music ... and see if the Holy Spirit brings you to new understandings of yourself, your community, and God.

> *"The most basic lesson that all art teaches us is to stop, look, and listen to life on this planet, including our own lives, as a vastly richer, deeper, more mysterious business than most of the time it ever occurs to us to suspect as we bumble along from day to day on automatic pilot. In a*

world that for the most part steers clear of the whole idea
of holiness, art is one of the few places left where we can
speak to each other of holy things." [1]

Labyrinth

Throughout the pandemic, Hagar's Community Church has moved around to different worshipping spaces around the Washington Correction Center as the chapel was turned into a temporary infirmary in case of a potential spread of the virus. For one period of time, HCC worshipped in the Visitors' Room. As the pastor, I loved getting to use the visit room—mostly because it was a large space we could use to do different creative practices. One week I decided that I would create a prayer labyrinth for the women. I brought in a bunch of Christmas lights, moved all the tables and chairs to the sides of the room, and designed a prayer labyrinth on the ground using the strings of little white lights. Because it was made with light, the labyrinth really stood out—it was beautiful. While I was shaping the lights into the labyrinth, officers kept calling and asking the chapel officer what was going on—and several officers walked over so they could give the labyrinth a try for themselves. In each of the six worship services that weekend, I taught the women about labyrinths and gave them time to walk it; the feedback I got was incredibly positive and heartwarming.

---

[1] Frederick Buechner, Whistling in the Dark: A Doubter's Dictionary (San Francisco: HarperCollins, 1988) p. 16.

Labyrinth at Okra Abbey, New Orleans, LA

I used this story to introduce Hagar's Community Church to walking a labyrinth:

> *In New Orleans at the Okra Abbey we had a labyrinth painted on the concrete and every Friday morning we held space for folks from the neighborhood to come and walk the labyrinth. One Friday morning I was at the Okra Abbey and it was my job on this particular morning to lead a labyrinth walk. I had the coffee ready, the cold water and I waited. It seemed that no one was interested ... until a guy from the neighborhood walked in. I knew him pretty well and it was clear to me that he was under the influence of something, but he walked up and we started talking and he asked me what the labyrinth was all about. I gave him a very simple overview (in my*

*head assuming he was too high to get anything out of it)
and then sent him on his way to walk it. He walked the
labyrinth for what seemed like an hour. He kept stopping
and kneeling ... and crying ... and praying. Some folks
walked in to get coffee and would ask what he was doing.
When he was done, he walked over to me and began to tell
me about his experience. In the following moments I was
astounded and convicted. I had thought this person had
nothing to teach me, but rather through his testimony he
taught me all that the labyrinth has to offer.*

-Pastor Layne

Create your own labyrinth using items around your house like
rope or Christmas tree lights! Use chalk to draw a labyrinth in
your driveway or in the streets of your neighborhood. Make
or buy a "finger labyrinth" if you don't have the space for a
full-size labyrinth. If there's a church parking lot nearby that
sits empty most days of the week, go knock on their door and
talk to them about painting a Labyrinth in the parking lot
that folks in the community can use to connect with their
spirituality. If you need help finding an outdoor artist in
your area to help you create a labyrinth, write us an email
at hagarscommunitychurch@gmail.com and we'll help you.
With most services being online, and considering that most
people attend church only on Sundays nowadays, a big, empty
parking lot may be a reminder of the good old days when the
parking lot used to be full ... but perhaps it is also the seed
of a new gathering. Perhaps the idea of worship is expanding
to include something sacred like gathering together outside
and centering ourselves—body, heart, mind, and soul—in the

spiritual practice of walking with the Lord.

How to draw your own finger labyrinth

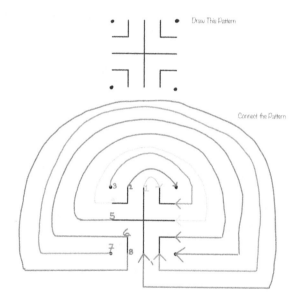

Prayer for Walking the Labyrinth

The holy season of Lent beckons us
  Toward sacredness and simplicity
  Toward deeper dimensions of faith
  And toward the holy mystery of God,
  Magnified in the life, death, and resurrection of Jesus

Christ.

During this season help us to seek peace O Lord.
Help us to seek out parks and labyrinths
And other quiet circles of grace
Where we can take an intentional walk together with you
Help us to be mindful of the ways your Spirit shows up in our lives
Whether we are walking in a labyrinth,
in the busy city streets, or way down a country road.
Amen.

Letter Writing

The dictionary says that an epistle is a letter or a poem in the form of a letter. In many ways, isn't writing someone a letter like writing a poem? Taking the time to pen a letter to a friend or even an enemy can be a very meaningful act. Letters can serve as a point of connection, as an act of prayer, as a document for the historical record, a canvas for meaning-making with words and so much more. How do *epistles* turn up in your life? When was the last time you wrote a letter?

One resource we recommend is Abolition Apostles, a national jail and prison ministry based in New Orleans, Louisiana. One feature of their ministry is prison pen-palling in order to "establish connections and offer moral support." Visit their website to become a pen pal and learn more about this important ministry (https://www.abolitionapostles.com/about).

Here's another idea: have ever written to your congressperson or even a local council member? If you have, what would you like to write to them now? Is there an issue in your community that you are passionate about and would like to support? Is there a civil servant you'd simply like to thank for their willingness to serve the community in a leadership capacity?

Last, but not least, our favorite letters usually come to us from those we hold most dearly in our hearts—often written with handwriting forever familiar to us. Think of someone dear in your life (family, friends, etc.) and consider sitting down to pen them a letter about what they mean to you and how much you love them. Don't be shy, just put pen to paper and let love loose.

Breath Prayer

The Hebrew word for "Spirit" is *"ruach"* which means "breath" or "wind." The Holy Spirit, the very presence of God, exists in our breath and in the breeze that ripples the waters and the leaves. Breath prayer is an ancient practice that combines breathing with short, memorable phrases. This practice integrates our mind and body and centers us in the present moment through breathing and repetition. If a phrase from scripture or from a prayer or poem in this book speaks to you, try praying it using a breath prayer! It's a wonderful way to *embody* the words in this book and prayer/scripture in general. See the example below and use this template to plug in whatever phrases or words are meaningful to you. Go slowly. Breathe deeply. Take it easy on yourself.

Inhale: *Be still*

Exhale: *Be-loved*

Praying a Daily Office

The practice of praying the daily office is the practice of choosing to center your life around prayer. It is setting out with the intention to have mini-meetings with God in the morning, midday, and in the evening. These mini-meetings with God are a keystone of an authentic relationship with the Holy One. Daily prayer is an integral part of all religions, not just Christianity. To pray means to participate in the mystery of the Divine—the Holy Spirit that spans across all time and space and connects all people as one through Jesus Christ.

As many of our daily routines have shifted and continue to shift, praying the daily office offers a simple way to center ourselves in prayer and scripture, an easy way to get in the habit of hanging out with the Holy One. May this spiritual practice center you in God's love, which is unchanging, as so much around us feels uncertain and ever-changing. Below you will find a template, an offering to help you practice the daily office. Please know that there are an abundance of resources out there. If this is something you'd like to explore further, be sure to research different books of common prayer and check out the myriad smartphone apps available.

Morning

Morning Prayer:

As the sun rises, we open our hearts to your grace anew, O Author and Artist of Creation! Let us rejoice that God is alive, that we are alive, and that God's Spirit is with us again today—and is here in this very moment—closer than our very breath. Amen.

Morning Scripture:

"Enter God's gates with thanksgiving; go into the holy courts with praise; give thanks and call upon the name of the Lord. For good is the Lord, whose mercy is everlasting; and whose faithfulness endures from age to age." (Psalm 100:4-5)

Midday

Midday Prayer:

Heavenly Mother, we pause and take time out of our day to give thanks to you. Thank you for walking with us, for loving us, and for calling us your children. Help us to see you in the face of all those we encounter throughout our day. We pray this in the name of the Mother, Son, and Holy Spirit. Amen.

Midday Song:

We are One in the Spirit, we are One in the Lord / We are One in the Spirit, we are One in the Lord / And we pray that our unity will one day be restored / And they'll know we are Christians by our love, by our love / Yes they'll know we are Christians by our love.

Midday Scripture:

"Dear friends, let us love one another, for love comes from God. Everyone who loves has been born of God and knows God. Whoever does not love does not know God, because God is love." (1 John 4:7-8)

Evening

Evening Prayer:

Sweet Jesus, Gracious God, we give you thanks for you tender mercies, for calling us your beloved. As the daylight comes to an end, we move forward into the night in peace, knowing that you hear us and you hold us in a constant state of grace. We praise you for your immeasurable love, O Lord. Amen.

Evening Scripture:

"You are my lamp, O Lord. My God lightens my darkness. This God is my strong refuge and has made my way safe." (2 Samuel 22:29, 33)

I

Seeking God

The First Week In Lent

1

Ash Wednesday: Blessed and Bound

"Let me hear joy and gladness; let the bones that you have crushed rejoice.

Hide your face from my sins, and blot out all my iniquities.

Create in me a clean heart, O God, and put a new and right spirit within me.

Do not cast me away from your presence, and do not take your holy spirit from me.

Restore to me the joy of your salvation, and sustain in me a willing spirit."

- Psalm 51:8-12

Repent! by C.B.

A day of repentance, a day of turning. For some, Ash Wednesday is a day for turning away from certain things or people or ideas or habits. For others it's a turning towards certain ideals, dreams, and goals—or maybe even certain people, like our neighbors, we may have been failing to check in on. Is there something or someone God is calling you to turn away from—or to turn towards? It is a spiritual question to consider along the journey. May your considerations of turning, of repentance, be blessed.

Watercolor by Anonymous

Reflection

In the midst of a global pandemic, what new (and perhaps strange) meaning does Ash Wednesday take on? What does it mean to mark ourselves with ashes and be reminded of our mortality—of our death—in the midst of all the death and grief that surround us?

As we face our mortality perhaps closer than ever before—*from dust we came and to dust we shall return*—we also remember our humanity. We mark ourselves with ashes, the sign of the cross on our fallible foreheads, blessing our bodies, and acknowledging that death will inevitably be a part of our life.

Children of God, in the in-between, between birth and death, is a life *lived.* Every morning is a new chance to further uncover and discover the gifts God has given and is waiting to unfurl before us. Each new day is a new chance to commit, together, as a beloved community, to the kingdom work that God calls us to: realizing God's dreams for creation here on earth as it is in heaven.

Modern Day Prophets by Tatiana

Do we see any parallels between Black History Month and Lent? I mean any at all? If we were to grind them down—both the sad and the celebratory aspects of these set periods of time, I think we would come to see the common thread that not only tethers, but intimately intertwines the two together; struggle into sacrifice.

There is no Black History Month without the cruel reality of struggle. Slavery was never a choice. Whether we are talking about Black African bodies or Brown Hebrew bodies these people were enslaved through violence, cruelty, subjugation, family separation and terror. Slavery was not an agreement that slaves entered into with their captors like, "Okay look guys, we definitely want to work for you ... for free though ... and we'll do as much manual labor as you say is fair ... " I mean, really, we don't ever enter into that kind of agreement (although nobody ever reads the "terms & conditions" nowadays, so maybe we do?). But in fact, what we can see in these eras of struggle is something else. The struggle for freedom has been a breeding ground ... for sacrifice. Unfortunately, some of these sacrifices have been to foreign gods and deities and self-serving mechanisms; while yet, there were those who made a sacrifice to end the oppression. These sacrifices were found in the form of obedient human flesh: Prophets.

In all likelihood many have not considered this (and some won't still), but those Black men and women that we celebrate throughout our modern history as civil rights leaders, they are modern-day prophets. Their words may not have begun with "Thus saith the Lord," but every bit of their actions spoke God's tremendous efforts to gain our attention and focus it on the work that God was doing on the margins. Every trip made on the Underground Railroad; every Freedom Ride through the South; and every march for equal education, equal pay, equal housing, and equal rights that made someone stand up and take notice that God's Kingdom is on the move. God gave these freedom fighters—these modern day prophets—a choice, and God gives us a choice as well. There is a struggle going on—are we going to choose to acknowledge it and sacrifice for it? Do we choose to stay in this legalistic pattern that continually justifies the systemic oppression of Black and Brown bodies in the name of "justice"? Did we not have One who came to bear the government upon His shoulders? To take our

6

struggle and be our Sacrifice?

Question

On this Ash Wednesday and in the movement for Black Lives—as our unarmed Black siblings continue being lynched at the hands of the police, disproportionately incarcerated across the nation, and unequally affected by COVID-19—what is yours to acknowledge? What is yours to sacrifice? What work is yours to do? *As you contemplate these questions, know that our great God of Justice has gone before you to help make a way.*

Prayer

God of life, death, and resurrection,
*   When my attitude grows rotten like fallen fruit from tree*
*   Create in me a clean heart, O God, and put a new and right spirit within me.*
*   When my spiritual well dries up and I thirst for you like plants amidst a drought*
*   Pour out your Spirit, make me like a watered garden whose streams never fail.*
*   When I am running too hot—life overloaded, hectic and imbalanced*
*   Help me to be still and remember who you are*
*   When I look into the mirror and fail to see a beloved child of God*
*   Remind me that I am a child of God—unconditionally loved by Jesus*

When I hold on to anger and hate, failing to open up and let things go

Gently nestle me open like a moonflower with the tender mercies of your spirit.

When resources are sparse and times are tough

Multiply the fishes and the loaves

Help us to know that just as you cloth the earth with grass

You will shelter and provide for each one of us—our Rock and our Redeemer.

Amen.

2

Thursday: Disrupting Shame

"If we say that we have no sin, we deceive ourselves, and the truth is not in us. If we confess our sins, he who is faithful and just will forgive us our sins and cleanse us from all unrighteousness."
  - 1 John 1:8-9

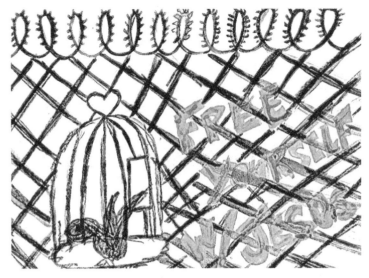

"Free Yourself w/ Jesus," watercolor by M.H.

Reflection

Sin is often accompanied by shame. Shame is a vicious cycle in which we believe we are inherently flawed and incapable of change because *it is who we are.* Brené Brown says that shame cannot survive being spoken out loud. It cannot survive being met with empathy. This is good news. We belong to a God who is faithful—whose grace covers all of our mistakes and defines us not by those mistakes but by our belovedness. When we speak our sin and shame and regret out loud, when it is met with empathy by a loving neighbor and a faithful God, we are then free to let it fall from our shoulders and move forward from a place of grace and gentleness. We are freed to repent, to turn a different way, to live out of a place of love instead of shame.

Question

When was the last time you felt like you "missed the mark"? When was the last time you showed someone empathy when they missed the mark? Practice disrupting shame with empathy by writing yourself a letter. Think of the last time you missed the mark and did or said something you regret. Confess onto the page. Now, practice showing yourself grace and forgiveness. Talk to yourself like you'd talk to a friend you love.

Prayer

> *Faithful God,*
> *thank you for never giving up on us*
> *and for continually seeking us.*
> *Remind us, when we show you the deepest*
> *and most shame-filled parts of ourselves,*
> *that we are not our worst mistakes but so much more—*
> *we are loved and forgiven and understood.*
> *Thank you for your grace.*
> *Amen.*

3

Friday: Spirit Eyes and Spirit Ears

"Lord, let your face shine upon your desolated sanctuary. Incline your ear, O my God, and hear. Open your eyes and look at our desolation and the city that bears your name. We do not present our supplication before you on the ground of our righteousness, but on the ground of your great mercies, O Lord, hear; O Lord, forgive; O Lord, listen and act and do not delay!"
- Daniel 9:17b-19a

"Hear Our Prayers," watercolor by Anonymous

"Grandmother, when you pray before the fire, are you listening?"

"The fire is a relative of the sun, the life giver. It helps me listen for the Great Spirit. When I pray I am listening ... with my spirit-eyes and my spirit-ears."

Rising Fawn looked at the fire. "I see flames. I hear them snap and roar. That is all."

"You are using your body-eyes and body-ears," said the Grandmother. With her finger she tapped Rising Fawn's chest. "You must listen with your spirit-eyes and spirit-ears."

"Can you teach me how to listen?"

The Grandmother shook her head. "All I can teach you is to be still. You must ponder the fire mystery for *yourself."*[2]

Reflection

God is not some divine Mr. Potato Head (or Mrs. Potato Head for that matter!). God does not have ears or eyes as we know them, but rather God has Spirit eyes and Spirit ears and spiritual senses that we can't even imagine! When the prophet Daniel says, "Incline your ear, O my God, and hear. Open your eyes and look at our desolation," Daniel is speaking spiritually. Jesus often speaks in such a spiritual way. In the Gospel of Mark chapter eight he says, "Do you still not perceive or understand? Are your hearts hardened? Do you have eyes, and fail to see? Do you have ears and fail to hear? And do you not remember?" The people's failure of spiritual perception is connected in some intimate and mysterious way to their hearts and their memories.

Question

Have you ever paused to imagine how your "spiritual vision" and your "spiritual hearing" are affected by memory and the habits of the heart? In what ways might a habit of prayer or participation in a worshipping community shape your spiritual eyes and your spiritual ears? It's curious how the choices we make today will be the memories we can recall tomorrow—each day a new lens—a fresh opportunity to hear and see what God will unfurl and unfold before us. A new day

---

[2] Marilou Awiakta, *SELU: Seeking the Corn-Mother's Wisdom*, (Golden Colorado: Fulcrum Publishing, 1993), p.75.

to see who God will put before us—someone to reach out to and love and care for, or perhaps someone who will reach out to and love and care for us.

Prayer

God,

You hear our whispers and cries in the night,
and each new morning you offer us tender mercies and a clean slate.
Through the unconditional love of Jesus,
we have the assurance that we never walk alone.
May this assurance give us spiritual eyes and spiritual ears
to see those who are lonely and in need of a friend,
to reach out to those who are hurting and need someone to talk to,
and to learn how to love ourselves
so that we can better love others the way you want us to.
We pray this all in the name of the Father, the Son, and the Holy Spirit.
Amen.

4

Saturday: When You Feel Broken

"While I kept silence, my body wasted away
through my groaning all day long.
For day and night your hand was heavy upon me;
my strength was dried up as by the heat of summer."
- Psalm 32:3-4

Eirene by Rachel

I am bereft of the ability
To be a maker of peace
For the inexplicabilities lie within
The realm of the unforeseen
Incarceration has broke me
Shattered my family who disowned me
Drowned me in guilt.
I speak the same words
King David spoke in his distress,
"My dishonesty within myself

Because of my unconfessed sins
Caused my life to be filled with frustration,
Irrepressible anguish and misery.
The pain never gave way,
For your hand, O Lord, of conviction
Was heavy on my heart ...
My strength was sapped, my inner life
Was dried up—like a spiritual drought
Within my soul."
For Jesus said to let Him restore the brokenness
Of our family,
for restoration redeemed the wounded soul.
God is Peace; the Prince of Peace
By His will and His way,
I need to let go and let God,
Although,
I feel I must be the bearer of this burden
Yet,
I must leave it to God
To be at peace
Within these walls.
To have Shalom within myself
And heal my wounded soul
And accept incarceration broke me
So that Eirene could save me.
For Jesus even said, "Just come with me."

Reflection

The writer of this poem speaks of personal and family brokenness and her inability to make peace on her own. She feels the burden weighing heavy yet she longs to give it all to God. Her strength is sapped and her throat dry.

There is a Japanese art called *kintsugi* where broken ceramics are mended with gold rather than being thrown out or replaced. The point isn't to make the dish not look broken; rather the fractures are filled with gold therefore making the repaired ceramic *more* valuable. Being broken becomes a part of the history of the object, rather than a blemish to be disguised.

"Ring the bells that still can ring / Forget your perfect offering / There is a crack, a crack in everything / That's how the light gets in." - *Anthem* by Leonard Cohen

Consider all of this when you feel broken.

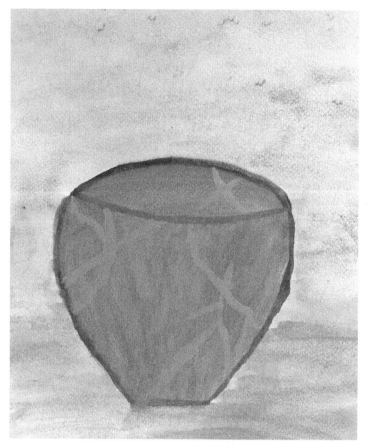

"Untitled," watercolor by Anonymous

Prayer

Divine One,
  for those who feel broken and shattered,
  like the weight of the world is on their shoulders,
  grant them glimpses of Shalom.

19

Remind them that they don't have to be healed to be
whole,
    and that every wound and pulse in their beloved bodies
    belongs to You.
    Amen.

5

First Sunday in Lent: Furiously Claiming Who We Are

"In those days Jesus came from Nazareth of Galilee and was baptized by John in the Jordan. And just as he was coming up out of the water, he saw the heavens torn apart and the Spirit descending like a dove on him. And a voice came from heaven, 'You are my Son, the Beloved; with you I am well pleased.' And the Spirit immediately drove him out into the wilderness."

- Mark 1:9-12

"Child of God, Holy and Beloved," watercolor by Anonymous

Reflection

One of the first things I did when I moved to Washington State to start Hagar's Community Church was attend churches in my new Presbytery. I was hungry to learn the culture, the land, and the language of this place. One of the churches that I attended was Bethany Presbyterian Church in Tacoma, WA, and a part of their weekly liturgy was a call and response: "Who are you? I am a child of God, Holy and Beloved." These words struck me and I couldn't stop saying the phrase over and over as I drove back to the Airbnb my husband and I were renting. At the first worship service of Hagar's Community Church I decided to use the liturgy I heard in the communion liturgy.

22

One Voice: *On this holy day let us remember that we are not who the world says we are —our Identity is deeper than that.*

All Voices: *I am a child of God, Holy and Beloved. At this Holy Table, we are reminded of who we really are.*

One Voice: *Friends, who are you?*

All Voices: *I am a child of God, Holy and Beloved.*

This liturgy became the beating heart of Hagar's Community Church. Throughout my time at the Washington Corrections Center for Women (WCCW) these words were not only repeated at every worship service but also gave definition and mission to the church. The mission of what we do at Hagar's Community Church is to always affirm that we are children of God, holy and beloved. We are not defined by the world, but rather who we are in relationship to God.

-Pastor Layne

Prayer

God,

As we set out on this Lenten journey, let us bring with us the knowledge, deep in our souls, that we are Yours and that You call us beloved.

At the same time, help us remember: our neighbor is a child of God too.

May we see all those we encounter along the road through Your eyes.

Amen.

II

Tears, Stories, and Other Holy Things

The Second Week In Lent

6

Monday: When Tears Appear, The Spirit is Near

"I cry aloud to God, aloud to God, that he may hear me. In the day of my trouble I seek the Lord; in the night my hand is stretched out without wearying; my soul refuses to be comforted. I think of God, and I moan; I meditate, and my spirit faints."
 - Psalm 77:1-3

"Tears are Prayers Too," watercolor by S.G.

Reflection

Tears are tough, but have you ever thought of tears as a sign of the Holy Spirit? Tears connect us as humans in so many ways—showing up in the eyes of those on both sides of wars, on both sides of divorce, in the eyes of humans on every continent who practice every faith imaginable. The One Spirit—the Holy Spirit that connects us all, is with us all, and moves through us all—is present in moments of tears. The Spirit is present in moments of deep joy and deep sorrow. *"Likewise the Spirit helps us in our weakness; for we do not know how to pray as we ought, but that very Spirit intercedes with sighs too deep for words."* (Romans 8:26)

Prayer

God of joy and sorrow,
When we don't have the words,
when we are beyond language,
may Your Spirit step in and communicate
Our deepest longings and fears.
May our tears be a sign of
Our connection to You
And to all of humanity.
Amen.

7

Tuesday: Frayed & Nibbled Survivor

"Finally, all of you, have unity of spirit, sympathy, love for one another, a tender heart, and a humble mind. Do not repay evil for evil or abuse for abuse; but, on the contrary, repay with a blessing. It is for this that you were called - that you might inherit a blessing....Now who will harm you if you are eager to do what is good? But even if you do suffer for doing what is right, you are blessed. Do not fear what they fear, and do not be intimidated, but in your hearts sanctify Christ as Lord."

- 1 Peter 3:8-9;13-15

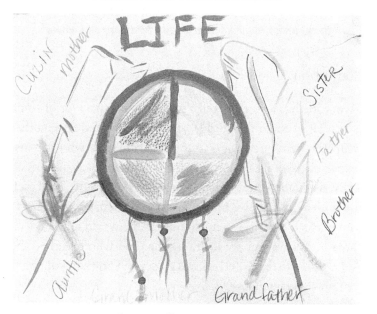

"Untitled," by Anonymous

Excerpt from *Pilgrim at Tinker Creek* by Annie Dillard

*"I am a frayed and nibbled survivor in a fallen world, and
I am getting along. I am aging and eaten and have done
my share of eating too. I am not washed and beautiful,
in control of a shining world in which everything fits,
but instead am wandering awed about on a splintered
wreck I've come to care for, whose gnawed trees breathe a
delicate air, whose bloodied and scarred creatures are my
dearest companions, and whose beauty beats and shines
not in its imperfections but overwhelmingly in spite of*

them, under the wind-rent clouds, upstream and down."[3]

Reflection

Everyone has a story to tell. Everyone is a survivor of some sorts. How might the world change if we treated one another with the gentleness we use to treat someone who has just experienced hurt or loss? Perhaps in some way we are all "frayed and nibbled survivors in a fallen world" and could each do with a dose of awe on our Lenten pilgrimage. So much is not perfect. There is so much hurt in the world. Take a deep breath. Know you are loved by the God who breathed the stars into existence and who is closer to you than your very breath—and be in awe.

Prayer

Gracious God—make us mindful.
   Mindful of our steps and mindful of our smiles
   Mindful of our time with You and when it's been awhile
   Mindful that we stop and rest and turn to You in prayer
   Ready to listen—arms wide open—tender loving care
   You are always there. You are always here—with us.
   Gracious God, make us mindful of Your presence in
the midst of it all.
   Amen.

---

[3]   Annie Dillard, *Pilgrim at Tinker Creek* (New York: HarperCollins, 1974), p. 245.

8

Wednesday: Jesus' Deprivation in the Wilderness

"Then Jesus was led up by the Spirit into the wilderness to be tempted by the devil. He fasted forty days and forty nights, and afterwards he was famished ... "
  - Matthew 4:1-11

"The Wilderness Road," pencil and ink by Anonymous

Reflection

Sensory Deprivation by Anonymous

When you're locked up you don't wear perfume. You don't smell the good things in life, and sometimes you have to spend time with people who may not shower as often as you do. You may have to eat foods that you've never eaten before, fruit that isn't ripe and often meals not even warm by the time you eat them.

Jails don't provide earplugs, white noise or mood music. You may be startled by sudden loud noises, distracted by someone's loud conversation, or taunted by repetitive, rhythmic, thumping or tapping. You won't be able to turn off the lights, night or day, and sometimes you might not have access to any natural light. You can't have a watch, and you might not be able to see a clock. It's disorienting. In some situations you might not know if it's day or night; if they're serving breakfast or dinner; if it's a weekday or holiday. You may not know the weather, the date, or the source of the sounds that you can't escape.

It was like that for me when I was segregated in jail. I had a deck of cards, pencils, and paper. I wrote to my family everyday. I had to tell someone about those circumstances. I lived in fear that they would take those few things I had from me too. That fear motivated me to "Hibernate." I decided to stop playing solitaire and writing letters. I focused my energy on becoming invisible. I wasn't hungry and the food wasn't appetizing. I limited my food consumption and lay on my bunk, eyes closed, arms at my sides and chose to deprive myself from my comforts ... in preparation for their loss. I focused my attention on me. I didn't feel hungry. Didn't miss food. Wasn't curious about who was outside my door.

When I awoke from "Hibernation" I had a fuller appreciation for my sensory experiences and a deeper rooted sense of understanding—of knowing that I could live with less.

Prayer

Lord of Mercy—to whom we cry out—help us to make room this Lenten season

Room in our hearts for You, and room at our table for others

Room in our day for You, and room in our budget for

others

Room in our evenings for You, and room in our prayers for others.

This Lenten season we remember Jesus' deprivation in the Wilderness

and we lift up to You—Lord of Mercy—Defender of the Outcast—

all those who are deprived of basic needs.

Have mercy on us as a society that champions wealth above meeting the basic needs of our citizens.

Help us to learn new ways to love God

with all our heart, mind, soul, and strength;

and to love our neighbors as we love ourselves.

Amen.

9

Thursday: Containing Multitudes

"The poor shall eat and be satisfied; those who seek him shall praise the Lord. May your hearts live forever! All the ends of the earth shall remember and turn to the Lord; and all the families of the nations shall worship before him. For dominion belongs to the Lord, and he rules over the nations. To him, indeed, shall all who sleep in the earth bow down; before him shall bow all who go down to the dust, and I shall live for him. Posterity will serve him; future generations will be told about the Lord, and proclaim his deliverance to a people yet unborn, saying that he has done it."

- Psalm 22:26-31

"Untitled," watercolor by Anonymous

Reflection

One would never guess that this beautiful passage of devotion to our Creator, the God of the Universe, comes from the very same psalm that begins with the famous words, "My God, my God, why have you forsaken me?" Encompassed in this one psalm are emotions that range from individual anguish to communal thanks and praise. Jesus cried out these words from the cross, and as he was hanging there in individual anguish, there was a community giving thanks and praise to be rid of him. The mob and religious leaders who had plotted to have Jesus arrested and crucified were glad to hear of Jesus' pain and suffering.

Those words from Psalm 22 were not the only ones Jesus

spoke from the cross that day. He also told the criminal hanging next to him, "Today you will be with me in paradise." Jesus was God, hanging there on that cross, dying for all of our sins. Our Creator, the God of the Universe, the very one who cried out "My God my God, why have you forsaken me?" is the same God who knows our pain and suffering. God calls us holy and beloved and is with us in the midst of it all.

Prayer

Alpha and Omega,
One who holds all the complex depths of human experience,
And is acquainted intimately with all our joys and sorrows,
Teach us to feel it all. Help us not to conceal our feelings, but to feel our feelings Lord.
Thank you for seeing us.
Thank you for knowing us.
For getting down in the hole with us,
So that we never have to feel whatever it is we are feeling alone.
Amen.

10

Friday: The God Who Hears

"The angel of the Lord found [Hagar] by a spring of water in the wilderness, the spring on the way to Shur. And he said, 'Hagar, slave of Sarai, where have you come from, and where are you going?'

'I'm running away from my mistress Sarai,' she answered.

Then the angel of the Lord told her, 'Go back to your mistress and submit to her.'

The angel added, 'I will increase your descendants so much that they will be too numerous to count.'

The angel of the Lord also said to her:

'You are now pregnant
and you will give birth to a son.
You shall name him Ishmael,
for the Lord has heard of your misery.
He will be a wild donkey of a man;
his hand will be against everyone
and everyone's hand against him,

40

and he will live in hostility
toward all his brothers.'"
- Genesis 16:7-12

"Hagar Runs," watercolor by Anonymous

Reflection

In the late Rachel Held Evans' retelling of the story of Hagar, she writes, "You may think a prophecy of struggle and strife would have disheartened a pregnant mother, but a slave does not struggle or strive; a slave only obeys. If the prophecy was true, it meant Hagar's child Ishmael, would be free."[4] The child would be free. Hagar, fleeing from the abuse of her master Sarai and close to death in the wilderness, is visited by an angel of God next to a well of water. The angel tells her that she will be a mother of a nation and her child will be free. The angel bears witness: God has *seen and heard her misery* and blesses her and her descendants in the midst of it all.

This sacred "seeing and hearing" shows up again and again in meaningful moments throughout scripture. In Exodus chapter three, the cries of the enslaved Israelites, God's own people, moves God towards action. Their cries of pain move God to deliverance and liberation. "Then the Lord said, 'I have *observed the misery of my people* who are in Egypt; I have *heard their cry* on account of their taskmasters. Indeed, I know their sufferings, and I have come down to deliver them from the Egyptians." (Exodus 3:7-8)

In the Gospel of Luke chapter seven, when John the Baptist sends messengers to ask Jesus if he is really the Messiah, Jesus responds: "Go and tell John what you have *seen and heard*: the blind receive their sight, the lame walk, the lepers are cleansed, the deaf hear, the dead are raised, the poor have good news brought to them. And blessed is anyone who takes no offense at me." (Luke 7:22-23)

What are we to make of the parts of Hagar's story without the angel? What of the hostility promised to her son Ishmael? What should we make of God telling Hagar to return to her oppressor? For that, we turn to Hagar. What stuns Hagar above all else—above the blessing and promise of both freedom and struggle—is that God has heard her cries and called her by

---

[4]   Rachel Held Evans, *Inspired*, (Nashville: Nelson Books, 2018).

name. The God of Sarah is now the God of Hagar too.

Prayer

God of All,
  We cry out to You and You hear us.
  Help us believe it is true.
  Send us angels and signs,
  Help us pay attention to the gifts
  You drop onto the doorsteps of our lives.
  Help us recognize the ordinary well of water
  As Your abundant aid and overwhelming mercy.
  Amen.

11

Saturday: The God Who Sees

"So [Hagar] named the Lord who spoke to her, 'You are El-roi,'[5] for she said, 'Have I really seen God and remained alive after seeing him?' Therefore the well was called Be'er-lahai-roi;[6] it lies between Kadesh and Bered. So Hagar bore Abram a son, and Abram gave the name Ishmael to the son she had borne."

- Genesis 16:13-15

---

[5] *El-roi* means "God of seeing," or "God who sees."

[6] *Be'er-lahai-roi* means "the well of the Living One who sees me."

"El-Roi," watercolor and ink by Anonymous

Reflection

Not only has God heard Hagar's cries, but God has seen her and she has seen God. Only one person in all of scripture dares to name God: her name is Hagar. Foreigner, woman, slave—cast aside and rendered invisible in her society. The folks at Hagar's Community Church inside of the Washington Corrections Center for Women hold Hagar's story close to their hearts. They know what it feels like to be erased from a story, to be sent away and no longer heard or seen. They also know that this story exists in our sacred text; they know Hagar, of all people, is the one who dares to name God. They find healing in knowing that in the midst of life God sees us and

45

uses our story to bring about God's plan for the world. God is not scandalized by our stories, but is right there in the midst of them. God was there in the wilderness with Hagar. God is there with the folks inside the WCCW. And God is here with you and me right now, full of tenderness, grace, and mercy.

Prayer

El-roi, One Who Sees,
    You see us, and You are not scandalized.
    There is nothing we can do to separate us from Your love.
    Thank you for seeing us. Thank you for loving us.
    (Or are they one in the same?)
    May we look for and listen to the stories
    Of those whom mass incarceration has tried to erase.
    And may their stories deepen and widen
    Our capacity for compassion and mercy.
    Amen.

12

Second Sunday in Lent: Furiously Burning It All Down

"If any want to become my followers, let them deny themselves and take up their cross and follow me. For those who want to save their life will lose it, and those who lose their life for my sake, and for the sake of the gospel, will save it."

- Mark 8:34-45

COME Follow Me . . . .

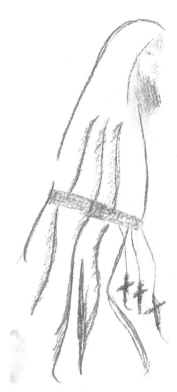

"Come Follow Me," pencil illustration by Anonymous

Reflection

What does a life with Jesus look like? What does it mean to follow Jesus? What do we expect? The disciple Peter had certain expectations about the Messiah: he was to be the one who would remove burdens and take away pain. So what do we do with a Messiah who says, "I'm headed to the cross, and here's yours!"? A life of faith isn't a fairytale; things aren't always going to go well. Sometimes it all falls apart with Jesus.

This text is asking us, *what have you lost and what will you have to lose for the sake of the Gospel?* It's asking us to sit in pain and grief. It's asking us to face the reality of death before we turn towards new life. Following Jesus doesn't mean a life without pain. A life with Jesus teaches us that before we walk in resurrection, we must sit in pain.

Question

What do you do instead of feeling pain? Busyness and productivity, numbing or repressing, distraction or avoiding, perfection and striving? What do you need to lose? What do you need to face?

Prayer

> *Cross-bearer and way-maker,*
> *We are so afraid of truly living the way You've called us to live.*
> *Stripped down. Open. Raw. Vulnerable.*
> *Layer upon layer of protection keeps us numb and out of touch with You.*

49

Give us the courage to let it all burn,
So that we may rise anew from the ashes of our life,
And enter into new life with You.
Amen.

III

Hagar and the God Who Sees

The Third Week In Lent

13

Monday: Teaching Each Other to See and to Laugh

*"Now Sarah said, 'God has brought laughter for me;
everyone who hears will laugh with me.' And she said,
'Who would ever have said to Abraham that Sarah would
nurse children? Yet I have borne him a son in his old
age.'"*
  - Genesis 21:6-7

An Experience by Rachel

I laughed today in a strange way
  It felt good I might say, in an uplifting way
  It tingled my toes, all the way to my nose
  Butterflies in my belly
  This feeling is kind of tight
  Considering the guilt, shame
  I've strangled to keep
  Happiness indeed, I feel it inside of me

When I look back on this night
I laugh, I know it's right
Then the tingling starts
From my nose to my toes!

Reflection

I often wonder how things could have been different if Sarah and Hagar had worked together and not fallen into the trap of jealousy and spite toward one another. Why *did* Sarah get jealous? Why *did* Hagar have contempt? What *if* Sarah had taught Hagar to laugh? What if Hagar taught Sarah to see? How would the story be different? Use your imagination - or perhaps your creativity - to envision what could have been.

I tell the women at Hagar's Community Church (HCC) that my prayer is that they might see each other the way God sees them - the way I see them - as living witnesses to the Living God. It is a stereotype of incarcerated people that they don't get along, that it is all fights, gangs, and violence. Now of course to some extent there is partial truth to the stereotype. Don't get me wrong, prison can be a rough and tough place. But at HCC we strive to be a place that welcomes folks to step outside of the stereotypes and mischaracterizations. HCC strives to create a unique space within the WCCW, one that affirms everyone's dignity and helps to bring down walls of division, a space that helps us to see one another how God sees us, and a space where we can laugh together.

-Pastor Layne

Prayer

Shine on us, O Light of the World,
  the secret sunshine of delight and wonder.
  Let it warm the earthen clay of our hearts from the
inside out
  and let it pour over our faces in smiles
  as we consider just how much You love us God.
  Let us smile in the safety of knowing
  that You have gone before us to make a way
  and You are by our side throughout the day.
  Amen.

14

Tuesday: Things Not Seen (or Felt)

"Now faith is the assurance of things hoped for, the conviction of things not seen. Indeed, by faith our ancestors received approval. By faith we understand that the worlds were prepared by the word of God, so that what is seen was made from things that are not visible."

- Hebrews 11:1-3

Pencil and Ink by Anonymous

Reflection

There is an unseen order of the Universe; there is a Divine Power greater than ourselves that we cannot put our finger on. It will always be the Great Mystery. The God who strung the stars in the sky and set the sun and moon in place is the same God who walks beside us, lives within us, and goes before us. When we look at the glistening night sky or watch the swirling colors of a sunset we are left with little doubt that God is at work, our God is a living God. And God is with us. When it is hard to feel God's presence in your life, remember: God's presence does not depend on us feeling it. Again, *God's presence does not depend on us feeling it.* God is at work and has gone before us to make a way for us. That is good news indeed.

Prayer

> *Ground of All Being,*
>   *May we be convicted, deep in our souls,*
>   *That You are the unseen element in all that we*
>   *Hear, feel, see, touch, taste.*
>   *Teach us to trust the You that exists within us*
>   *And within all of our creation.*
>   *Help us to Know.*
>   *Amen.*

15

Wednesday: Light in the Living Room

"Then he brought Israel out with silver and gold, and there was no one among their tribes who stumbled. Egypt was glad when they departed, for dread of them had fallen upon it. He spread a cloud for a covering, and fire to give light by night. They asked, and he brought quails, and gave them food from heaven in abundance. He opened the rock, and water gushed out; it flowed through the desert like a river. For he remembered his holy promise, and Abraham his servant. So he brought his people out with joy, his chosen ones with singing. He gave them the lands of the nations, and they took possession of the wealth of the peoples, that they might keep his statutes and observe his laws. Praise the Lord!"

- Psalm 105:37-45

Living room prayer station

Reflection

When I read this passage of scripture it makes me think about a time I was in the wilderness and God showed up in a very real way to provide for me and Hagar's Community Church. For a year and half I had been working at the Washington Correction Center for Women (WCCW) to establish and develop Hagar's Community Church. All of my energy had been going into creating rhythms and practices that this new congregation could live into. Two core pillars of the community included gathering every Saturday for Worship as one large body of faith and sharing communion during that service. From one Saturday to the next, all of that evaporated when the news of the Pandemic hit and a whole new reality was established.

March 7th, 2020 was the last worship service with HCC before the Covid-19 health crisis. The following week was when everything started changing. Washington's Governor Inslee restricted groups to remain under 50 people and everyone began to retreat into their homes to shelter in place and social distance. On that Thursday, I received notification from the WCCW that all programming was cancelled and I would be notified when I could return. I was permitted by the prison to send worship resources to the women but for two weeks I had no communication with any of my congregants. During the two weeks I had no idea how long the separation would last and my biggest fear was being shut out for the remainder of the year.

Prayer became a staple for me. I created in my living room a prayer station full of candles that became a place to channel all of my worries, fears, and hopes. I also reached out to the growing community of people who support and love Hagar's Community Church on the outside and asked people to join me in prayer. I told the women of HCC through the worship resources I was sending out to join me in praying every day at 5:00. Those of us on the outside began virtually meeting on Saturdays at 5:00 to pray for ourselves and for all the women incarcerated at the WCCW. On the evening of March 25th I was feeling incredibly hopeless. I had heard nothing from the WCCW and so in a quiet moment of desperation I lit every candle at my prayer station. Every candle was a prayer for Hagar's Community Church, a prayer that I would get a sign from God about the future. The next morning, I received an email from the WCCW; God answered my prayers. After a two week quarantine there were no cases of Covid-19 at the WCCW and the administration wanted to discuss what going forward with smaller in person worship services might look like.

-Pastor Layne

Watercolor, by Anonymous

Prayer

> *Holy God,*
> *When we find ourselves in the wilderness*
> *and are desperate to be found,*
> *Give us eyes to see all the ways you provide for us.*
> *When we are desperate and cry out for help,*
> *surprise us with your unexpected grace.*
> *Amen.*

16

Thursday: It's Not Too Late to Hope

"Once you were not a people, but now you are God's people; once you had not received mercy, but now you have received mercy."
- 1 Peter 2:10

He Spoke by Rachel

Suddenly it came
   Tears slowed, sobbing stopped
   Looking up to the dove in the
   Window
   The warm, heavy, forgiving embrace
   Welcoming me
   Instead of remorse, fear, regret,
   I felt hope
   Instead of shame, purpose
   It's not too late to hope
   God speaks

In that still, small voice
That could be so easily ignored
So often forgotten, dismissed
He reminds you to whom you
Belong
And with that reminder comes
Floods of determination
And courage to do something
About it

Reflection

In his book, *Just Mercy*, Byran Stevenson says:

"There is a strength, a power even, in understanding brokenness, because embracing our brokenness creates a need and desire for mercy, and perhaps a corresponding need to show mercy. When you experience mercy, you learn things that are hard to learn otherwise. You see things you can't otherwise see; you hear things you can't otherwise hear. You begin to recognize the humanity that resides in each of us."[7]

There's something about the knowledge that we belong to God. Perhaps it is this knowing, that each of us is a child of God holy and beloved, that moves us to show compassion and mercy when we could punish or hurt back.

And when the world is cruel, when individuals and systems

---

[7] Byran Stevenson, *Just Mercy: A Story of Justice and Redemption*, (New York: Spiegel & Grau, 2014), p. 290.

use their power to punish and break, there is something about knowing that we belong to a God who is described in our sacred text, over and over again, as merciful and gracious, slow to anger and abounding in steadfast love and faithfulness. Our hope is in the One who sides with the oppressed and the mistreated. May we be ones who receive God's mercy and who show mercy to the very people we've been taught to hate or ignore.

Prayer

Merciful God,
Whisper in our ears and remind us,
like the writer of the poem we read today,
That it is not too late to hope.
The world is cruel and corrupt,
but we find our wholeness in You.
Help us to practice hope.
Move us to compassion and mercy,
Remembering that we belong to You
And so does everyone else.
Amen.

17

Friday: Intentions of the Heart

"Let the words of my mouth and the meditation of my heart be acceptable to you, O Lord, my rock and my redeemer."

   - Psalm 19:14

Acrylic Painting by Anonymous

Reflection

If you've ever attended a Protestant church it is likely you have heard a pastor pray these words from Psalm 19:14 before preaching their Sunday sermon. I know one pastor who prays a variation of this, saying, "May the words of my mouth and the mediation of my heart rise up and be glorifying to you - and if these words are not of you today, Jesus, let them fall away and be forgotten."

I love this prayer. It gets to the heart of this verse in the Psalm - may all that we say and all that we long for and act upon be aligned with God, who is within us and present with us in every moment.

I wonder...what if before we started each day, we lifted up

these words from Psalm 19 to God? *"Let the words of my mouth and the meditations of my heart be acceptable to you O Lord, my rock and my redeemer."*

In a prayer by Thomas Merton, he says, "I believe that *the desire* to please you does in fact please you." Merton highlights here that God cares about the intentions of the heart. God cares that we try, that we love kindness, and long to do justice and humbly walk alongside our God. God knows and cares about the intentions of our hearts. We will never be perfect and we will always mess up. Will we ever let ourselves receive grace and *really* believe that God meets us and loves us just the way we are?

Prayer

by Thomas Merton

> *My Lord God, I have no idea where I am going.*
>   *I do not see the road ahead of me.*
>   *I cannot know for certain where it will end.*
>   *Nor do I really know myself,*
>   *and the fact that I think that I am following your will*
>   *does not mean that I am actually doing so.*
>   *But I believe that the desire to please you does in fact*
> *please you.*
>   *And I hope I have that desire in all that I am doing.*
>   *I hope that I will never do anything apart from that*
> *desire.*
>   *And I know that if I do this you will lead me by the*
> *right road,*
>   *though I may know nothing about it.*

Therefore will I trust you always,

though I may seem to be lost and in the shadow of death.

I will not fear, for you are ever with me,

and you will never leave me to face my perils alone.

Amen.

18

Saturday: Bread of Life

"Six days later, Jesus took with him Peter and James and John, and led them up a high mountain apart, by themselves. And he was transfigured before them, and his clothes became dazzling white, such as no one on earth could bleach them. And there appeared to them Elijah with Moses, who were talking with Jesus. Then Peter said to Jesus, "Rabbi, it is good for us to be here; let us make three dwellings, one for you, one for Moses, and one for Elijah."

- Mark 9:2-5

"A New Covenant of Abundant Grace," acrylic painting by
Anonymous

Reflection

I have always considered the transfiguration to be a *wild* story...
and it is one of the texts that I as a preacher struggle with -
what is going on here? Why did Jesus just pick two people?
Why did Jesus become all sparkly? Why did ghosts appear?
I don't have answers to this. Rather, it is just a mystery I am
asked to sit with each year on Transfiguration Sunday. But I
have been thinking about a time when Jesus was transfigured
for myself - not quite the same experience as the disciples, but
rather Jesus as the bread at the communion table. Communion
was transformed for me at the first worship service of Hagar's
Community Church.

71

At our first official worship service, only two other women and I gathered for worship. When it was time to share communion I realized that I had brought way more bread than was necessary for three women. So off the cuff I told the two women, "Feel free to take as much as you like, since you can never have too much of Jesus!" Both of their eyes grew large and I watched as they both pulled off huge hunks of bread. Then they carefully dipped their bread in the grape juice and we sat together in silence for about five full minutes eating our communion bread. Eventually one of them broke the silence and said, "Wow, we never get bread like that!" We all laughed a bit and then said our final communion prayer together.

In reflection I realized that I had never before had communion with a community that needed the nourishment of the Bread of Life as much as these women did. I thought back to all the times I have offered communion in churches not in a prison, typically when people come forward they take the smallest piece possible off the loaf. I'm not really sure why this is the typical practice among most Christians. Fear of taking too much, fear of eating too many carbs, or maybe people just aren't as hungry for the Bread of Life. But week after week it has been my greatest joy to offer communion to the women of Hagar's Community Church and to watch them take generous hunks of bread and be fed by Jesus Christ who is truly the Bread of Life.

So what began as an off the cuff joke - you can never have too much of Jesus - has now become the foundation of our time together each week. I tell my congregation it is my goal for them to experience the abundance of God's love for them in the extravagance of the bread.

-Pastor Layne

Prayer

Bread of Life,
Give us today our daily bread.
Give us what we need to survive and thrive
During this ordinary day on earth.
Transform our senses so that the ordinary
May be signs of Your Love.
We cannot live by bread alone,
But by Your Spirit.
Your presence,
In the elements of our daily living.
Amen.

19

Third Sunday in Lent: Furiously Flipping Tables of Oppression

"In the temple he found people selling cattle, sheep, and doves, and the money changers seated at their tables. Making a whip of cords, he drove all of them out of the temple, both the sheep and the cattle. He also poured out the coins of the money changers and overturned their tables. He told those who were selling the doves, 'Take these things out of here! Stop making my Father's house a marketplace!'"

- John 2:14-16

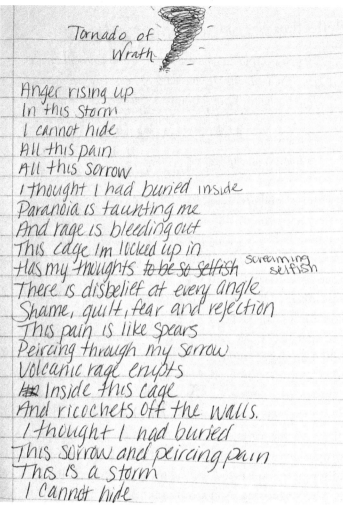

Tornado of
Wrath

Anger rising up
In this storm
I cannot hide
All this pain
All this sorrow
I thought I had buried inside
Paranoia is taunting me
And rage is bleeding out
This cage I'm locked up in
Has my thoughts ~~to be so selfish~~ screaming selfish
There is disbelief at every angle
Shame, guilt, fear and rejection
This pain is like spears
Peircing through my sorrow
Volcanic rage erupts
Inside this cage
And ricochets off the walls.
I thought I had buried
This sorrow and peircing pain
This is a storm
I cannot hide

"Tornado of Wrath" by Rachel

Reflection

"If you want to do violence in this world you will always find the weapons. If you want to heal, you will always find the balm. With scripture, we've been entrusted with some of the most powerful stories ever told. How we harness that power, whether for good or evil, oppression or liberation, changes everything."[8]

It's almost embarrassing to admit this but the image of Jesus erupting in anger, flipping tables and driving people out of the temple is one of my favorite images of Jesus in the Bible. As someone who has a temper and has had to learn time and time again to control my own anger... it sort of feels as though this image of Jesus gives me permission to feel all that anger I sometimes experience.

Anger is a tricky emotion. It is common for people to say "Oh, I don't get angry.... I just get frustrated sometimes." We are taught to be fearful of our anger, that anger can ruin us or cause us to do things we will regret- and therefore we 'should' avoid it at all costs. One of my Seminary Professors said in class "no one has ever died from feeling a feeling, but plenty of people have died from not feeling them." It took me a couple of different therapists to finally allow myself to feel all the anger I had been ignoring. And how thankful I am that I found a great one who gave me permission to feel my feelings - permission to be angry!

What I learned is that anger can serve as a signpost to point out when something in my soul needs to be tended to. Anger

---

[8]   Rachel Held Evans, *Inspired*, (Nashville: Nelson Books, 2018), p. 57.

can be destructive, but anger can also be a wellspring of life. It can be the energy I need to say no to something that is hurting me, it can be a sign that justice is not being served- that it's time to step up and be an advocate. Anger can be a hot destructive fire burning everything around it, but I have learned if I allow myself to feel my feelings as they arise (rather than trying to stuff them back down) - that fire never becomes all encompassing. Thank you Jesus for your willingness to show us that anger is an important expression of our faith.

-Pastor Layne

Prayer

Help us God,
   to learn together as a community to walk in your ways
   of peace and humility rather than our own ways of
pride and violence.
   We turn to you in prayer and you point us to your
amazing grace,
   where radical forgiveness is found.
   Lord,
   let your amazing grace transform our community.
   Let our community be transformed by your amazing
grace.
   Sweet Jesus,
   let your Kingdom come - where swords are beaten into
plowshares
   and guns are transfigured into garden tools
   and tanks are transformed into tractors.
   Bless our hands,
   touch our hearts,

move our feet
and walk always with us this day and every day.
Amen.

IV

A New Church Mosaic

The Fourth Week in Lent

20

Monday: Holy Bodies of the Church

"Do you not know that you are God's temple and that God's Spirit dwells in you?"
  - 1 Corinthians 3:16

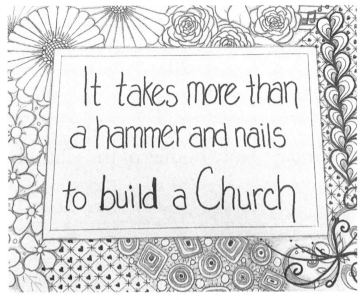

"It Takes More," pencil and ink by Anonymous

Reflection

Once upon a time there was a nursery rhyme that went something like this: "Here is the church, here is the steeple, open the doors, and see all the people!" It's cute, but it's misleading. For you see, if you examine the nursery rhyme closely, it suggests that "the church" is something other than "the people." But the Apostle Paul does not say, "Do you not know that that building with a cross on it is God's temple?" but rather, "*You* are God's temple and … God's Spirit dwells in you." And in the Gospel of John, Jesus does not say, "On that day you will know that I am in my Father, and you in me, and I in a building." No! Jesus says, "On that day you will know that

I am in my Father, and you in me, and *I in you.*"

God is in you. God is closer to you than your very breath. "Do you not know that you are God's temple and that God's Spirit dwells in you?" What does this say about our bodies? If we take this spiritual truth seriously, maybe it means that our minds and our hearts and our thighs and our toes ... that *all* of us is *holy.* The women of Hagar's Community Church know all too well that a church is not defined by a steeple or stained glass, but that church can be found and created behind barbed wire and metal bars. Church can also spring up in urban gardens, skate parks, and living rooms. Church is in me and church is in you. We—the people—are God's church, holy and beloved, called to share the Good News.

Prayer

Dear Lord,

today we give you thanks for church community
for a group of fellow believers
where we can practice things like faith, hope, and love,
confession, forgiveness, and reconciliation.
Thank you for the gift of others:
the diversity of humanity that reveals
just how extraordinarily beautiful and complex you
are
mysterious and merciful God
intimate and incarnate Lord.
Help us to reach out to those who are isolated and
lacking community
and continue to be open to meeting new people,
making new friends,

and learning new things.

We pray this all in the name of the Father, Son, and Holy Spirit.

Amen.

21

Tuesday: My Heart and My Flesh Sing (and Dance and Cry)

"How lovely is your dwelling place, O Lord of hosts! My Soul longs, indeed it faints for the courts of the Lord; my heart and my flesh sing for joy to the living God. Even the sparrow finds a home, and the swallow a nest for herself, where she may lay her young, at your altars, O Lord of hosts, my King and my God. Happy are those who live in your house, ever singing your praise."
  - Psalm 84:1-4

Excerpt from *Beloved* by Toni Morrison

"After situating herself on a huge flat-sided rock, Baby suggs bowed her head and prayed silently. The company watched her from the trees. They knew she was ready when she put her stick down. Then she shouted, let the children come!" and they ran from the trees toward her.
    Let your mothers hear you laugh," she told them, and

the woods rang. The adults looked on and could not help smiling.

Then "Let the grown men come," she shouted. They stepped out one by one from among the ringing trees.

Let your wives and your children see you dance," she told them, and groundlife shuddered under their feet.

Finally she called the women to her. "Cry," she told them. "For the living and the dead. Just cry." And without covering their eyes the women let loose."

It started that way: laughing children, dancing men, crying women and then it got mixed up. Women stopped crying and danced; men sat down and cried; children danced, women laughed, children cried until, exhausted and riven, all and each lay about the Clearing damp and gasping for breath. In the silence that followed, Baby Suggs, holy, offered up to them her great big heart.

She did not tell them to clean up their lives or to go and sin no more. She did not tell them they were the blessed of the earth, its inheriting meek or its glory bound pure.

She told them that the only grace they could have was the grace they could imagine. That if they could not see it, they would not have it.

"Here," she said, "In this here place, we flesh; flesh that weeps, laughs; flesh that dances on bare feet in grass. Love it. Love it hard."[9]

---

9   Toni Morrison, *Beloved,* (New York: Random House, 1987), pp.102-103.

Reflection

When I was allowed back into the prison to conduct worship after the COVID-19 shutdown, I was so excited. I thought we were so lucky to have in-person worship services for Palm Sunday. My illusion was quickly shattered when I started considering all the ways that the pandemic would affect our time together. Singing had become dangerous and was not allowed anymore. I would have to wear a mask at all times, which meant I would have to try to preach with a mask on. The one large worship service I normally lead on Saturday nights would now have to be split into nine separate worship services spread out over Friday, Saturday, and Sunday in order to keep everyone safe. This really put a damper on the excitement of in-person worship! All of the sudden everything changed, worship services included.

I began to rethink what it would mean to gather in worship as one community. This is when art became a central component to the worship life of our time together. When the women gathered, I played worship music and gave them the opportunity to express their faith through art: painting, drawing, writing poems and notes of encouragement to one another. At the end of the worship service they hung their creations on the walls of the chapel so that those gathering during the later worship services could see their messages of hope.

It was a small way of communicating the connectedness of our worshipping community even in the midst of so much distance and separation.

The pandemic has presented an opportunity for the Church to rethink the ways we do things. It has offered us a chance to use our imaginations to open up what a worship service looks like and what it means to "gather together." When was the last time you laughed in church? When was the last time you danced? When was the last time you sat in silence longer than the sermon? And why not? None of these things are any less sacred than singing or preaching. Maybe, just maybe, the pandemic is an opportunity for the Church to cherish our bodies, to not take ourselves for granted, and to really figure out how to use *all* of our body, mind, and soul in worship as we engage the creative arts.

-Pastor Layne

Prayer

Lord of Dance,
   infuse us with joy and whimsy.
   Shape us into more daring and loving creations.
   Grant us play and laughter,
   especially in the spaces we've been taught to be serious
and quiet.
   May we express our worship and our faith through our
bodies—
   through singing,
   laughing,
   dancing,
   weeping,
   embracing.
   Amen.

22

Wednesday: A Pilgrim's Path

"Happy are those whose strength is in you, in whose heart are the highways to Zion. As they go through the valley of Baca they make it a place of springs; the early rain also covers it with pools. They go from strength to strength; *The God of gods will be seen in Zion. O Lord God of hosts, hear my prayer; give ear, O God of Jacob!"*
  - *Psalm 84:5-9*

"A Walk In the Rain," acrylic painting by L.B.

Reflection

Psalm 84 is the song of a pilgrim people whose hearts were set on Jerusalem, the place where the holy Temple Mount found its home. Religious festivals often involved a pilgrimage to this holy city. Can you imagine the excitement and awe of walking towards the temple and finally seeing it rise over the hill after a long, hard journey of having your heart set on this sacred destination? Yet the Psalm does not say, "Happy are those whose strength is in the *temple*," but, "Happy are those whose strength is in *you*." Visiting the temple was not so much about the place, but about the *presence of God*.

What if we thought about our lives as a pilgrimage? We walk with God through the dry valleys, finding springs of nourishment that have collected in those low places along the hard way. We walk with God atop the majestic mountaintops, breathing in the fresh air and feeling the weight of the world fall off our shoulders, gathering the strength we need to make it through the next low place. *We go from strength to strength*, gaining an ever-increasing comprehension of God-with-us, our hearts set not on a destination, but on the One who journeys with us.

Prayer

> *Ever-present Guide of our journeys,*
>> *Thank you for being our constant companion*
>> *And friend along this hard road we call life.*
>> *Thank you for all the times you've quenched our thirst in the desert,*
>> *All the times you've shown up when it wasn't rainbows and sunshine.*
>> *Give us the strength we need to be present on our own pilgrim path,*
>> *Tuned into You, gently guiding us to the next right thing.*
>> *Set our hearts on You, the One we follow.*
>> *Amen.*

23

Thursday: People of the Rainbow

"When the bow is in the clouds, I will see it and remember the everlasting covenant between God and every living creature of all flesh that is on the earth.' God said to Noah, 'This is the sign of the covenant that I have established between me and all flesh that is on the earth.'"

- Genesis 9:16-17

"All Are Welcome," watercolor by Anonymous

Reflection

Prior to the covenant and the appearance of the rainbow in Genesis chapter 9, God was grieved by how humans were inclined to violence. It pained God to see the disorder and evil inclinations of the creation God loved so much. There was a problem. The flood was God's solution to this problem—a drastic solution, no doubt—but prior to the covenant and the rainbow, a flood was what God saw fit to restore order to the chaos that had arisen.

Sometimes when people talk about "Noah's Ark" and the flood, they make it sound like God started all over. But there's another reading that's more true to the text. The flood wasn't God's decision to start over with humanity or creation (otherwise why would there be a Noah and an ark?). The flood didn't fundamentally change the human condition; it didn't fix some primordial problem with our souls. No. In the flood, God decided to work with us *as we are.* This is how God works. God saw there was a problem and God worked with Noah, his family, and a bunch of creatures crammed into an ark for 40 days and 40 nights to bring about a new beginning, a fresh start. This was grace.

When the flood subsided, God reestablished the order of creation. The rainbow became the sign of the covenant between God and all living beings. God longs for humanity's flourishing and for the rest of creation's flourishing too! The theology of the rainbow is that each of us is charged with working to create conditions in which all humans and living beings can flourish. Ponder and accept this charge, knowing that God works with us *just as we are.*

Prayer

God of floods and rainbows,
  Open our eyes to injustice.
  Stir up energy in us to work with you
  To create a world where all can love, flourish, and live
well.
  Thank you for your never ending grace.
  Amen.

24

Friday: Laughter in Church

"O give thanks to the Lord, for he is good; for his steadfast love endures forever. Let the redeemed of the Lord say so, those he redeemed from trouble and gathered in from the lands, from the east and from the west, from the north and from the south."
  - Psalm 107:1-3

"Lily of the Prison Yard," acrylic painting by Anonymous

Reflection

One night (before COVID-19 was a thing), Crawford and I were leaving worship at Hagar's Community Church. As we were walking out of the chapel, an officer commented that it was surprising and unique to hear so much laughter during the worship service. He said, "It's not that often that the women get to laugh together." As we drove home we began to process what the officer had said. It was so different from our experience at the prison. I can honestly say that the worship services I have the honor of leading each week are some of the most laughter-filled worship services I have ever experienced. This is not to say that they are not taken seriously by the congregation or that they are making fun of worship. Rather, there is so much joy in the room. Smiles and laughter become almost contagious! Folks in my congregation come eager to participate in worship, to fellowship with one another, to praise God and to share prayer requests about what is happening in their lives. Even when the updates are hard or disappointing, they turn to each other, eager for the comfort of friendship and community.

The members of Hagar's Community Church have taught me that laughter is a signpost pointing me towards what is most sacred and most holy. This comment by the officer helped me understand a bit more of my calling at the WCCW. I see myself holding space each week for the women to come together and experience joy: their own joy and the joy that their Creator takes in them.

What Hagar's Community Church has shown me is that when you need the joy of God, you just have to be willing to open your eyes to see it and trust your community enough to experience it.

-Pastor Layne

Prayer

Almighty God,
Imaginative Creator of the Universe, Source of Life,
help us, we pray, to pause and take a step back during this Lenten journey
in order that we might regain a perspective of your grand design for Creation.
As we come to the doorstep of Spring,
startle our senses, Sweet Jesus.
As buds of life burst forth from the dead of winter and the natural world begins to be born again,

slow us down, Lord,

that we might stop and smell the Lavender,

the Lilac, and the Lilies of the Valley.

Creative Creator, you know how we hunger for Spring

for you created within us a spiritual understanding of seasons,

of rhythms, of the way life moves not in a line but rather in circles.

You created within us the capacity to hope,

to change, to grow, to die, and to live again.

Point us in these days of Lent to the holy cycle of life, death, and resurrection.

Help us to live our lives as humble songs of Your extraordinary love.

Inspire us with your Holy Spirit.

Instill in us a new conviction to live and not just to survive.

Help us to believe again in miracles and lead us in relationships and service

whereby we participate *in Your miracles, O God.*

We give you all our thanks and praise.

Amen.

25

Saturday: Born of Water and Spirit

"Very truly, I tell you, no one can enter the kingdom of God without being born of water and Spirit. What is born of the flesh is flesh, and what is born of the Spirit is spirit. Do not be astonished that I said to you, 'You must be born from above.'"

  - John 3:5-6

"Christ's Mercy Rains," acrylic painting by Anonymous

Reflection

In January 2020, the worst possible thing happened. Right as the group was gathering for worship, a fight broke out between two women in attendance. It was, for me, an unsettling event and one that I did not get over quickly. My congregation offered me words of assurance saying things like, "It wasn't your fault," "It happens," and, "Don't worry about it." But after that, I could not help but be hyper-vigilant. I jumped at every little movement, struggling to find any sense of calm within myself.

A few weeks later, we had a celebration of baptism. 16 Incarcerated Individuals had taken a class in preparation for baptism, and now they were going to be baptized. And not with the typical Presbyterian sprinkles! They all wanted to be baptized in the giant, full immersion tub.

Despite all the anxiety I had experienced the previous several weeks, that night, I entered the kingdom of God through water and Spirit. As each woman went down and came up out of the water, the joy expressed on her face joined with the cacophonous clapping and whooping from the congregation and the singing of Sam Cooke's version of *Amen* to create a truly joyous affair.

I left that evening having experienced healing. I had not forgotten the fight, but it was no longer the only thing I could think about. The joy outweighed the sorrow. The dancing called us into a new community. The water and the Spirit ushered in the kingdom of God.

-Pastor Layne

Prayer

Inspired by Rev. Pattie Kitchen

> *Teach us, O Lord,*
>> *in the midst of a multitude of noise, to trust in You.*
>> *In the angry fussing of a fight,*
>> *In the sometimes sacred sounds of music,*
>> *In the often uncertain sound of the news of the day.*
>> *Teach us, O Lord,*
>> *in the midst of a multitude of noise, to trust in You.*
>> *In the whining of a child with unmet needs,*
>> *In the giggling of old women in the middle of Bible Study,*
>> *In the passing humming of someone with a song on their heart.*
>> *Teach us, O Lord,*
>> *in the midst of a multitude of noise, to hear you and to trust in You.*
>> *Amen.*

26

Fourth Sunday in Lent: Furiously Receiving Grace

"For God so loved the world that he gave his only Son, so that everyone who believes in him may not perish but may have eternal life."

   - John 3:16

"His Compassion," ink and acrylic illustration by V.G.

Reflection

John 3:16 is a text that many people know well. It has been popularized through signs at sporting events and concerts, and perhaps some know it so well that it's lost some of its impact and meaning. For some folks, the idea of a Father sacrificing his Son in the name of love isn't the most beautiful image, or the best way to imagine the atonement achieved through Christ's sacrifice on the cross. Scholars refer to such images as atonement theories, the reconciliation between a sinful humanity and a holy God through the sacrifice of Jesus Christ. While there are a variety of atonement theories, most of them have been written by white males who tend to write, think, and imagine from a place of privilege.

But what happens when we look at the crucifixion of Jesus through the eyes of some of the most marginalized people among us? How does this verse take on new meaning when we read it through the experience of a person in prison?

Let's put ourselves in the shoes of someone being punished for a wrong. Perhaps the image of Jesus taking on the punishment that we deserve could take on new meaning. Christ, who died for *our* sins, whose grace is bigger than our mistakes, is *good news* for us. We are no longer defined by our sin but by our identity in Christ: beloved, forgiven, and whole.

Prayer

You encourage Me...

Your compassion filters
all the struggles I am
given. Lord your love granted
me peace. your sacrifice
implanted me with hope, your
grace enriched may soul with faith.
You strengthen me when I
am weak. Created in your
image, how could I ever
lose?

Written by V.G.

V

With Us in the Wilderness

The Fifth Week in Lent

27

Monday: Practicing Hope in the Wilderness

"Then Moses ordered Israel to set out from the Red Sea, and they went into the wilderness of Shur. They went three days in the wilderness and found no water. When they came to Marah, they could not drink the water of Marah because it was bitter. That is why it was called Marah. And the people complained against Moses, saying, 'What shall we drink?' He cried out to the Lord; and the Lord showed him a piece of wood; he threw it into the water, and the water became sweet."

- Exodus 15: 22-25

"Untitled," watercolor by Z.R.

Reflection

In the midst of a hard season of wilderness, I had a wise mentor say to me, "All is not lost." When I'm in a place of anxiety, I often cannot see the light at the end of the tunnel. I worry things will be this way forever, or I jump to the very worst-case scenario.

Her words were simple but they have stayed with me, on my heart, since that day. They remind me of my faith in a faithful God who provided for the Israelites in the wilderness and who provides for me in mine. It encourages me to practice hope.

Practicing hope, for me, comes from a place of faith. Because God has shown up in the past, I know God will show up again and again. When I can't see the light at the end of the tunnel, when the water has run out and I can't fathom how I will ever take a drink again, I remind myself that all is not lost. God will show up in surprising and unexpected ways because God has done so before, and God is faithful.

Question

The wilderness is a place of contradictions. In the wilderness we experience the anxiety born from uncertainty, the pain of grief and the disorientation of newness. It can also be a place of freedom, of leaving old ways behind, and of encountering God and discovering gifts to sustain us along the way.

What does the metaphor of wilderness mean for you right now? What is hard? What may be the gifts? What does it mean for you to practice hope in the wilderness?

Prayer

Creative Creator, Sweet Jesus,
  give us the creative energy to practice
  and proclaim hope with our daily lives and living.
  Infuse us with Your Holy Spirit
  that we might let our little light shine wherever we may
go.
  As we continue to prepare our hearts for Holy Week,
  may You inhabit both the joy of our preparations
  as well as any lingering fears we may have
  with holy wonder and assurance of Your strong presence.
  Release us from prisons of doubt and feelings of unworthiness
  into the freedom of your unconditional love and forgiveness.

Thank you for being with us in the wilderness,
for protecting us, and for being the firm foundation of
our hope.
Amen.

28

Tuesday: Why, God?

"Now there was no water for the congregation; so they gathered together against Moses and against Aaron. The people quarreled with Moses and said, 'Would that we had died when our kindred died before the Lord! Why have you brought the assembly of the Lord into this wilderness for us and our livestock to die here? Why have you brought us up out of Egypt, to bring us to this wretched place? It is no place for grain, or figs, or vines, or pomegranates; and there is no water to drink.' Then Moses and Aaron went away from the assembly to the entrance of the tent of meeting; they fell on their faces, and the glory of the Lord appeared to them. The Lord spoke to Moses, saying: Take the staff, and assemble the congregation, you and your brother Aaron, and command the rock before their eyes to yield its water. Thus you shall bring water out of the rock for them; thus you shall provide drink for the congregation and their livestock."

- Numbers 20:2-8

"Water from the Rock," painting by Anonymous

Reflection

In my role as Re-entry Pastor for HCC, something I've heard consistently from folks who have just gotten out of the WCCW and are in the re-entry process is that while they wouldn't choose to go back, a part of them misses prison because life on the outside is just as hard, but in different ways. They often ask questions like: Why would God bring me out of the wilderness to just bring me to another wilderness?

While God doesn't create suffering or ordain the oppressive systems of this world, God never promised this life would be easy or without pain. God *did* promise to be with us, especially to be with the oppressed and the forgotten. God promised to work in the midst of it all. God promised that in the midst

114

of suffering and pain and struggle, seeds would be planted and that new life would blossom. God promised to provide in unexpected and surprising ways.

The Israelites had the same question: Why would you bring us out of the oppression of Egypt only to bring us into this desolate place with no food and no water? The wilderness wasn't easy, yet God showed up. God walked with them. God sustained them with springs of water and manna along the hard road. All the while, the land of milk and honey—the promised land—waited for their arrival.

-Pastor Riley

Prayer

Provider God, God-with-us,
   We are lost, we are overwhelmed;
   we are hurting and tired and scared.
   You tell us you are with us.
   We know from our sacred stories and from our own experience
   That this is true.
   That you show up in unexpected ways, through surprising people and places.
   Tune our eyes and ears so that we recognize your presence.
   Sustain us through the wilderness.
   Give us the hope of a promised land.
   Lead us there.
   Amen.

29

Wednesday: Everlasting, Ever-Present Light

"The sun shall no longer be your light by day, nor for brightness shall the moon give light to you by night; but the Lord will be your everlasting light, and your God will be your glory. Your sun shall no more go down, or your moon withdraw itself; for the Lord will be your everlasting light, and your days of mourning shall be ended."

- Isaiah 60:19-20

Pencil illustration by Sai. "We all have these defects that keep us from seeing the light to guide our way. It isn't until we get brave enough to reach out that we realize the light has been there the whole time." -Sai

Reflection

There's a quote my mom has shared with me at just the right times in my life, typically when I find myself in the midst of what feels like some form of catastrophe. It goes something like this: "It wasn't until my barn burned down that I could see the moon." I've been missing my mom in the midst of this pandemic. The women of HCC know all too well the pain of missing loved ones in the midst of this catastrophe as all visitations have been cancelled and on hold since the pandemic took hold here in Washington state in March of 2020.

The Prophet Isaiah says, "Who needs the sun and the moon? You will have the Lord as your everlasting light!" Jesus in the Gospel of John affirms the prophet's words saying, "I am the Light of the World! Whoever follows me will never walk in darkness but will have the light of life." It is a deep and abiding truth that the loving light of our God shines from everlasting to everlasting, but it is also a deep abiding truth that to be human is to suffer, to face catastrophe and grief, and there is darkness in that.

Try and picture a full moon bathing a wide open field on an early spring evening. In the middle of that field is an old, beat-up barn. There are birds swooping through the silver moonlight and crickets calling out to one another under its glow. The glory of the Creator is apparent in this place. But there is one sullen person sitting in the field in the shadow of the barn. This person is in fact so sullen, so caught up in a downward spiral in their own head, that they are blind to the beauty of the beaming full moon hiding just behind the barn.

Suddenly a racket arises from the barn, startling the person from their loneliness and causing them to get up and see what the fuss is all about! Hearing the "Hoo! Hoo!" of an owl, they move to the side of the barn, now in view of the full moon, just in time to see the gorgeous owl glide away under the glistening light of the full moon.

Catastrophes come and go, but the Word of the Lord—the Love of God—is from everlasting to everlasting. Like the Prophet Isaiah says, the Lord will be our everlasting light, and until that day comes don't sit sullen in the shadows of the barn when there's a field full of creation calling out to you, "Come frolic with us in the moonlight!"

Prayer

O Lord,
   who comforted the afflicted and afflicted the comfortable,
   Startle us from ourselves, that we might turn to You.
   Tear down what is preventing us from seeing Your light in our lives.
   Let us bask and dance in the delight of discipleship, O Light of the World.
   And may we let our own light shine everywhere we go.
   Amen.

30

Thursday: Listen to Your Life

"You desire truth in the inward being;
therefore teach me wisdom in my secret heart.
Purge me with hyssop, and I shall be clean;
wash me, and I shall be whiter than snow."
- Psalm 51: 6-7

Will It by Tatiana

Like a child, the natural reaction within
Is to tense up and refuse the change
Afraid of what this new is
And what it does.
Will it hurt? Will it
Bring me pain? Will it
Take away the small comfort already known?
Will it. Will it. Will it.

Fists holding sand, clenching nothing really

The delusion of control, secular facades
Of what life is all about.
Not unlike children, the imagination runs rampant,
Playing illusions of lives not meant to be lived,
Desires setting eyes aflame, lust and greed
Winnowing in the belly's depth
And still fear lingers.
Will we lose control?
Will it
Be taken away?
Will it all be for nothing?
Will it. Will it. Will it.

God said all it requires is child-like faith
  To knock down walls and walk on water,
  To cast down strongholds and draw out demons,
  To stand firm against addiction, divorce, sensuality,
  Anger, gluttony, false reality—the war being raged
  Is in the mind—alone.

Believe to release
  Believe to free
  Believe to live
  Believe to Believe to Believe to
  Sacrifice all the cords bound up
  So tight around the soul.

Reflection

The most wonderful part of our secret heart is that it cannot be analyzed or studied or figured out. It is just that—a secret! It is a fathomless mystery. The work that God does in our secret heart every day is unknown to us, but we experience the effects: the incremental changes in our daily life when we walk with God, when we talk with God, when we spend time with God, when we surrender to a Power greater than ourselves.

It may be hard to notice our growth in the moment, but when we look back over our lives and see the bigger narrative, the dots connect and we can take inventory of how far we've come. Take some time today to reflect on your own personal timeline, your own spiritual journey. Maybe even draw one out, noting milestones, pivotal decisions, life changing events or moments. Reflect on the wisdom you've gained and give God thanks for the surprise blessings that manifested from what may have at first begun as places and spaces of pain. Be in awe of the way things have unfolded, for better or for worse, the way God has loved you right to this very moment, and the way God is going to go on loving you each and every day no matter what. Be in awe.

> *"Listen to your life. See it for the fathomless mystery it is. In the boredom and pain of it, no less than in the excitement and gladness: touch, taste, smell your way to the holy and hidden heart of it, because in the last analysis all moments are key moments, and life itself is grace."*[10]

---

[10] Frederick Buechner, *Listening to Your Life,* (HarperOne, 1992).

Prayer

Gracious God,

Protector and Comforter,

Savior of the Lost and Disheveled, of the Honest Seeker and the Confused Wanderer;

we bow in our hearts this Lenten day

and take inventory of our hearts and our relationship with You.

We long for an authentic relationship with you, God, where questions are safely asked and faith restored.

Help us to place our trust in You by day and seek refuge in you by night.

Be our Calm, we pray, in the midst of confusion.

We bring to you, O Lord, the gifts you have given us to use,

the passions You have given us to refine,

the minds You have given us to cleanse,

and the hearts You have given us to be your home.

By the power of your Holy Spirit,

may Christ dwell in our hearts through faith

as we are being rooted and grounded in love.

Amen.

31

Friday: Freedom Fighter

"Since, then, we have a great high priest who has passed through the heavens, Jesus, the Son of God, let us hold fast to our confession. For we do not have a high priest who is unable to sympathize with our weaknesses, but we have one who in every respect has been tested as we are, yet without sin. Let us therefore approach the throne of grace with boldness, so that we may receive mercy and find grace to help in time of need."
- Hebrews 4:14-16

Reflection

The Ultimate Freedom Fighter By Tatiana

As we began Lent this year in the midst of Black History Month, and given the state of our country and world in the midst of this global pandemic, it is vital that we step back and see the ways that through our struggles and sacrifices we have walked the path of discipleship. God looked upon this world through a magnanimous and merciful lens and called it *good*—and after creating humanity God said it was "very good."

Jesus to some is a mere man and prophet. But to those of us who believe, Jesus is the One worth sacrificing everything for. Why not? God led our ancestors out of slavery and into the Promised Land. The Holy Spirit spoke words of liberation through prophets of old and continues to speak them today. Jesus died on the cross for our sins.

God continues to nourish us, a country that is slowly tolerating growth. In February, we celebrated Black History and our beloved Freedom Fighters; let us not forget the Ultimate Freedom Fighter, the Man who chose to become a man, who chose to dwell among us and bear our burdens, who took on the sins of every human being that ever lived to the point that Jesus became somehow unrecognizable and his Father, our God, had to look away from Christ's final moment in which struggle became sacrifice to free us.

Just as we celebrate and remember where we came from as Black bodies in america[11] in February, let us *never forget* where our saving hope comes from. Let us never forget who God is, and let us never forget that we are the beloved of the Ultimate Freedom Fighter.

Prayer

By Tatiana

> *Gracious Father,*

---

[11] America is left uncapitalized on purpose.

Embrace us as we embrace you.
We are not helplessly fighting
against racism, sexism, religious and cultural persecu-
tions alone,
for You are ever-present.
The journey for freedom is long,
but you, our great God of liberation and incarnation,
are with us every step of the way.
Whenever we forget about you, God, remind us.
Remind us of your sacrifice, and of your love,
and of your presence with us in the midst of it all.
Amen.

32

Saturday: God Uses Our Broken Hearts

"O Lord, open my lips,
  and my mouth will declare your praise.
  For you have no delight in sacrifice;
  if I were to give a burnt offering, you would not be pleased.
  The sacrifice acceptable to God is a broken spirit;
  a broken and contrite heart, O God, you will not despise."
  - Psalm 51:15-17

Pencil illustration by Anonymous

Reflection

In so many ways, the congregants of Hagar's Community Church have had to sacrifice everything they hold meaningful. To challenge them to give up anything else just seems irresponsible.

With that said, God has used such difficult and hard situations for good, and it never stops surprising me when sometimes I hear folks at the Correction Center tell me that they are thankful for their time in prison because of how that time has helped form them to be the person they are today. A broken heart is loved and used by God. The system that does the breaking is not good, but God is. The folks of HCC are resilient. In an environment that breaks, they have remained whole by the power of the Spirit and through the shared love of community.

When it comes to sacrifice, let us ponder this question: What if those of us with privilege sacrificed a little more so that those of us on the margins could sacrifice a little less?

Prayer

> *Bread of Life,*
> *the True and Untamed Vine, Word Made Flesh,*
> *Living Water, Prince of Peace, Son of God and King of Kings,*
> *We give you thanks today for finding us back here, in prayer,*
> *stirring our hearts for your Kingdom.*
> *Sweet Jesus,*
> *the sacrificial lamb who offered himself up to die for*

our sins,

the Light of the World that overcame the darkness of death,

the Lion of Judah and the Lamb of God,

the Sower, the Good Shepherd, Divine Healer, Doctor of Mercy,

the One who directs choirs of angels

and sends Your Holy Spirit forth to direct choirs of people praising God,

Love that we long for,

Hope that we hope for,

Peace that we pray for,

be with us and bless us this day and every day.

Amen.

33

Fifth Sunday in Lent: Furiously Learning How to Die

"Jesus answered them, 'The hour has come for the Son of Man to be glorified. Very truly, I tell you, unless a grain of wheat falls into the earth and dies, it remains just a single grain; but if it dies, it bears much fruit. Those who love their life lose it, and those who hate their life in this world will keep it for eternal life.'"

- John 12:23-25

Awe of Agony by Rachel

My heart is heavily guarded, my sorrow is a heavy chain
My tears they burn my face, consumed by the faceless darkness
Diluted as rain is to fire.
My eyes so sore from seeing, heavy like with 10 pound bricks.
My conscious is discarded garbage, it's almost as if ...

I have to cut out my heart ... and see it ... beating
  As though I have to learn how to die, before I can live.
  This pain that is my life keeps me from trying again.

Reflection

Throughout the Gospels, Jesus uses plant metaphors to teach us—fig trees, grains of wheat, mustard seeds. In today's text, Jesus reminds us that unless the grain of wheat dies, it remains the same. However when it dies, it bears fruit—it produces newness. When we are afraid of pain, afraid of the wilderness, we resist growth and block the flow of new life. The writer of the poem is in the very heart of pain. Notice words like "sorrow," "heavy chain," "tears," "burn," "consumed," "darkness," "sore," "discarded garbage." She is on a journey of learning how to sit in agony, to gaze upon it and move through it. Learning how to die so that she can live.

Seeds, Fruits, and Holy Garments by C.

> *A seed grows inside a cherry that hangs from a stem on a branch on a tree on a summer's day. The fruit acts as a holy garment for the seed such that a fellow member of creation—a bird perhaps—will recognize the seed for what it is: a holy offering. The seed—hanging there on the stem on the branch on the tree—dressed so pretty in its bright red, holy cherry garments—serving as a sign and symbol of love from the Creator in the form of nourishment for those in need.*
>
> *Suddenly, a bird in need alights upon the tree. The bird bows upon the bough and plucks the cherry—takes*

flight and carries it away.

The fruit—once a holy garment for the seed—has now become nourishment for those in need.

Prayer

Holy God,

Move with us through the thresholds of life,
be with us in both darkness and light.
Plant the seeds of light and new life
in the darkness of our lives.
Water and nourish these seeds with words of mercy;
reminding us that we are Your beloved children
and You walk with us and these seeds of new life
as a mother holds her child's hand when they cross the street together.
When seeds turn into sprouts,
and sprouts of new life begin popping up in our lives,
help us to nourish these new beginnings
and make room in our garden for all of Your beautiful creation.
Amen.

VI

Storytelling with the Holy Spirit

The Sixth Week in Lent

34

Monday: A Surprising Witness

"Bring forth the people who are blind, yet have eyes, who are deaf, yet have ears! Let all the nations gather together, and let the peoples assemble. Who among them declared this, and foretold to us the former things? Let them bring their witnesses to justify them, and let them hear and say, 'It is true.'

You are my witnesses, says the Lord, and my servant whom I have chosen, so that you may know and believe me and understand that I am he. Before me no god was formed, nor shall there be any after me. I, I am the Lord, and besides me there is no savior. I declared and saved and proclaimed, when there was no strange god among you; and you are my witnesses, says the Lord."

- Isaiah 43:8-12

Acrylic painting by Anonymous

Reflection

Pre-pandemic, every Saturday evening a small group of folks from local congregations in our Presbytery would join us for worship. Very often the group was composed of folks who had never been inside a prison before. When I would meet them at the entrance to escort them to the chapel, they would often have a look in their eyes that said, "I have no idea what to expect."

Almost 100% of the time when I was escorting the group out at the end of the night the conversation would be, "I think I just experienced what real worship should be like," or, "I never knew church could be so joyful!" Because this conversation was so common I thought a lot about what truth they were getting at. I think these visitors were witnesses to active work of the Holy Spirit, and it sure is exciting to see God at work!

   -Pastor Layne

Prayer

The Prophet Isaiah writes,

   "O people of Zion, inhabitants of Jerusalem, you will weep no longer.

   God will surely be gracious to you at the sound of your cry;

   When God hears it; God will answer you."

   - Isaiah 30:19

Children of God,

   Rest assured that God's promises are true.

   Our mourning shall be turned into dancing,

   and if you know where to look,

   you might just discover that the dancing has already begun.

   Ever-loving God,

   give us faith to trust your promises

   and eyes to see where you are calling us

   into new and unpredictable places of joy.

   God of incomprehensible compassion,

   embrace us with your grace

   and lead us with kindness into your calling for our lives.

   Amen.

35

Tuesday: You Cannot Take My Dignity

"In the last days it will be, God declares,
  that I will pour out my Spirit upon all flesh,
  and your sons and your daughters shall prophesy,
  and your young men shall see visions,
  and your old men shall dream dreams.
  Even upon my slaves, both men and women,
  in those days I will pour out my Spirit;
  and they shall prophesy."
  - Acts 2:17-18

Acrylic painting by Anonymous

Reflection

At the heart of the Pentecostal movement—at the heart of Pentecost—is the idea that God's Spirit moves and can speak through anybody. Anyone can be a voice for God. Reading this passage from Acts 2, "I will pour out my Spirit upon all flesh," I cannot help but reflect back on the Pentecostal tradition that raised me. My Pentecostal roots have provided me with a certain openness to the Spirit's moving in different contexts and settings. I'm ready and willing to hear God's voice speak from people who are often overlooked or aren't "allowed" to speak for God.

There is a common tendency to think we are bringing the Gospel to the incarcerated, but in reality these incarcerated women teach me.

Their knowledge of the Bible is profound. They see the text differently because of their life circumstances. I am blinded by privilege to certain theological concepts that they can see clearly. For example, we were discussing Ephesians 6, a Pauline prison epistle, in a Bible study. In the text, Paul talks about being clothed by a breastplate of righteousness and other spiritual garments.

One woman pointed out that in prison even your clothes don't belong to you; Paul was writing this while looking at a Roman prison guard. He was saying, "You can take my rights, you can even take my clothes, but you cannot take my spiritual garments. You cannot take my faith, my dignity, the things that make me a human in relationship with God."

By allowing fear and distance to keep us separated from our siblings of Christ in prison, we are depriving the larger Church from God's voice.

-Pastor Layne

Prayer

Spirit of the Living God, fall afresh on us today.
   Melt our hearts where they have hardened against those in need;
   Melt our voices when they rise in unjustified anger;
   Melt our wills when we stubbornly try to control outcomes
   that need to be placed in Your hands.
   Upon any staleness of faith that lurks in our souls
   or stumbles cynically from our lips,
   Melt our souls that we might rest in the cocoon of Your

grace.

Mold us, Almighty God,

that we might be some semblance of a holy people.

Sometimes we simply are not sure what holiness looks like,

or sounds like, or feels like,

and so we pray that You will mold us in myriad ways to work Your will.

Fill our hearts with burning questions of faith born in You.

Spirit of the Living God, fall afresh on us today.

Amen.

36

Wednesday: Treasure These Words

"I treasure your word in my heart,
so that I may not sin against you.
Blessed are you, O Lord;
teach me your statutes.
With my lips I declare
all the ordinances of your mouth.
I delight in the way of your decrees
as much as in all riches.
I will meditate on your precepts,
and fix my eyes on your ways.
I will delight in your statutes;
I will not forget your word."
- Psalm 119: 11-16

Acrylic painting by Anonymous

Reflection

The Psalmist, speaking to God, says, "I treasure your word in my heart." What does that mean, to treasure someone's words? Are there words that are treasures to you? Does "treasuring words in your heart" mean you like them and think they are special, the way Bruno Mars "treasures" that special someone he sings about? Or does it mean something else?

In a spiritual context, what does it mean to treasure God's word in our hearts? These questions are worthy of much discussion that cannot be had here in this book, but one practical suggestion is to consider memorizing some of God's Word.

Memorizing scripture can teach us to slow down, to focus

in on one text and take the time to internalize it. When we memorize God's Word, we tattoo it on our hearts so that it's always there whenever we might need it. We write it on our hearts because we treasure it.

Below we've included a short list of scripture references if you need a place to start. Keep these words on your heart so that you may remember God's love and God's call. Carry them around like mental furniture, so that you may turn to them in moments of need and rest.

- Lamentations 3:21-23
- Micah 6:8
- Matthew 6:19-21
- Matthew 7:1-5
- John 14:18, 27
- Romans 8:38-39
- 2 Corinthians 5:14-15
- Ephesians 3:14-21

Prayer

Loving God,
  may Your words be written on our hearts
  and sealed in our minds
  to be a strength and comfort in times of need.
  May our lives become so intertwined in Your Word
  that all we do is aligned with your loving purposes for
us and for all of creation.
  May our living bring your Kingdom just a little closer
to earth.
  Amen.

37

Thursday: Every Tongue Shall Confess

"Let the same mind be in you that was in Christ Jesus,
who, though he was in the form of God,
did not regard equality with God
as something to be exploited,
but emptied himself,
taking the form of a slave,
being born in human likeness.
And being found in human form,
he humbled himself
and became obedient to the point of death—
even death on a cross.
Therefore God also highly exalted him
and gave him the name
that is above every name,
so that at the name of Jesus
every knee should bend,
in heaven and on earth and under the earth,

and every tongue should confess
that Jesus Christ is Lord,
to the glory of God the Father."
- Philippians 2:5-11

Acrylic painting by Anonymous

"Lift Up Our Hearts and Our Tongues Shall Confess" by Anonymous

Lift up our hearts, we pray, O Lord, and our tongues shall confess of your glory.

Lift up our hearts above fear and doubt, and lift up our voices in song.

Lift up our hearts above logic—above our minds And into Your irrational, unconditional love and grace.

Lift up our hearts above anxieties of illnesses out of our hands that hover in the night and up into faith in You, O Lord, that You work all things for good for those who love You. There is nothing that can separate us from your love.

Lift up our hearts, we pray, and help us to love you with all of our heart, all of our soul, all of our strength, and all of our mind, and help us to love our neighbors. And Good God Almighty, help us to love ourselves!

Prayer

Sweet Jesus,

Dwell with us and within us here and now, that we may go forth from gathering here with You at this spiritual well of renewal with the light of hope in our eyes,

the fire of inspiration on our lips,

Your Word on our tongue and Your Love in our hearts.

We pray this all in the name of God who is One in three,

the Trinity: Father, Son, and Holy Spirit.

Amen.

38

Friday: Jesus Saves, Not Me

*"Therefore, my beloved, just as you have always obeyed
me, not only in my presence, but much more now in
my absence, work out your own salvation with fear and
trembling; for it is God who is at work in you, enabling
you both to will and to work for his good pleasure."*
  - Philippians 2:12-13

Patience by C.

Grant me patience, O Lord, in ways I have not known
  The patience of an Oak Tree that was once an Acorn
  The patience of an inch worm journeying a flower bed
  The patience of a gardener preparing the soil
  To plant seeds for a hopeful harvest
  The patience of a pastor preparing a sermon for Easter
  Putting in months of prayer before ever putting pen to
paper.
  The patience and steadfast faithfulness of Jesus

Fasting in the desert with the angels and the devil.

Patience like Moses and Martin who journeyed along-side their people in the wilderness

Patience like those who are imprisoned and yet persist

In speaking out for justice for the poor, the disenfranchised and the oppressed.

Transfigure slowly, O Lord, this patience into Your work.

May it grow into the fruits of Your Spirit, O God,

And may I feed and be fed, nourish and be nourished.

Colored pencil illustration by L.S .

Reflection

That phrase, "work out your own salvation with fear and trembling," is somewhat mysterious and a little bit … entirely frightening! Work out *my own* salvation? Some days I forget to take a shower or I don't even feel like getting out of bed. Work out *my own salvation*—are you kidding me?! I don't believe in that. What I believe is that *Jesus* saves, not me.

So I searched further into what "working out our own salvation" could mean and this quote came to mind from theologian and mystic Simone Weil about the Christian's search for Truth:

> *For it seemed to me certain, and I still think so today, that one can never wrestle enough with God if one does so out of pure regard for the truth. Christ likes us to prefer truth to him because, before being Christ, he is truth. If one turns aside from him to go toward the truth, one will not go far before falling into his arms.* [12]

That wrestling with God—that working-it-out, that struggling, and praying, and doubting, and crying, and cursing, and searching, and searching, and searching—that's what Christ wants. Because Jesus wants your heart, just as it is, in the midst of all that working-it-out—for God is right there in the midst of it all.

---

[12] Simone Weil, *Waiting for God*, (New York: HarperCollins, 1951), p. 27.

Prayer

Lord,
Give us patience in our struggle, in our wrestling.
Remind us that everything is temporary
and that Your mercies are new every morning.
Turn our mourning into praise.
Remind us that the wrestling and the doubting and the
struggling
are faithful acts of a walk with You.
Help us to keep the faith.
Amen.

39

Saturday: Family Tree of Eternal Life

"The days are surely coming, says the Lord, when I will fulfill the promise I made to the house of Israel and the house of Judah. In those days and at that time I will cause a righteous Branch to spring up for David; and he shall execute justice and righteousness in the land. In those days Judah will be saved and Jerusalem will live in safety. And this is the name by which it will be called: 'The Lord is our righteousness.'"

   - Jeremiah 33:14-16

Acrylic painting by Anonymous

Reflection

The Prophet Jeremiah speaks of a "righteous branch" spring-ing up. But whoever thought of branches as righteous or unrighteous? Can you imagine someone looking at a tree and saying, "Well, that branch there near the top looks honest and principled, but that lower branch seems quite immoral." It is silly to describe branches as having some sort of conscious or moral mark, but the Prophet Jeremiah is not describing a tree growing out of the ground. Rather, he's describing a branch on a family tree.

Family trees are complicated and have so many different branches, so many different stories, so many different histories, and—by the grace of God—so many new beginnings. Again and again, old branches are pruned and new branches spring up. The patchwork of life is sewn together with stories of heartbreak and love. This "righteous branch" that Jeremiah speaks of will later be King Jesus himself, descended from the anointed line of King David. There are folks in Jesus' lineage, in Jesus' family tree, that most people would describe as the rockstars of the Hebrew Bible; Judah, Jacob, Isaac, and even Abraham are part of the tree from which the branch of Jesus springs forth.

But wait. There are also some ... shall we say ... not so righteous branches in Jesus' family tree! The point here is *not* to do a deep dive into Jesus' family tree (but if you'd like to, go check out the scandalous stories of King Solomon the Polygamist [1 Kings 11:3], King Manasseh the Pagan [2 Kings 21:2], or King David the Adulterer [2 Samuel 11:2-5]), but rather to say that family trees are complicated—even the tree of "the righteous branch that springs up for David."

It is not our job to live up to some family member's expectations of who we *should* be. It is not *our* work to redeem the sins of our family's past. That is impossible, for Christ is our redeemer, not ourselves. Family roots run deep, and so does the pain of fractured bonds of trust, safety, and love between a family. Christ is our redeemer. When we abide in Jesus we are adopted as God's children and grafted into the Family Tree of Eternal Life.

In Jesus' last gathering with his disciples before his betrayal and arrest, he says to them,

> *"Abide in me as I abide in you. Just as the branch cannot bear fruit by itself unless it abides in the vine, neither can you unless you abide in me. I am the vine, you are*

158

the branches. Those who abide in me and I in them bear much fruit, because apart from me you can do nothing."
  - John 15:4-5

Prayer

Creative Creator God of changing seasons and unchangeable grace,

Today, in this moment, we lean upon your Everlasting Arms of Love.

When tender green shoots raise their bulbous heads above winter's barren ground,

we feel the sure return of growth,

a reflection in the natural world of Divine hope.

Where hopelessness has crept into our lives,

we pray for renewal through the tender winds of your Spirit.

Sweet Jesus, where violence attempts to extinguish hope,

we pray boldly that You would intercede

and inspire yet unimagined paths for peace.

And, Lord, where weariness and tension

have crept into the places we live and our personal relationships,

free us to love and to forgive,

knowing we are cradled in Your tender and merciful care.

Amen.

40

Palm Sunday: Fruit Born of Vulnerability

"So they took branches of palm trees and went out to meet him, shouting, 'Hosanna! Blessed is the one who comes in the name of the Lord— the King of Israel!' Jesus found a young donkey and sat on it; as it is written: 'Do not be afraid, daughter of Zion. Look, your king is coming, sitting on a donkey's colt!'"

- John 12:13-15

"Hosanna in Technicolor," by Anonymous

Reflection

On Palm Sunday of 2020, about a month after lockdown due to COVID-19, I scribbled these words in my journal:

> *"Meaning is everywhere, but what does it all mean? Now is the time for the priests and the poets, the writers and the artists to help us see, to help us make meaning, to help us fashion that which is meaningful, to remind us of who we are and who we were created to be, to help us deconstruct and reconstruct what is valuable to us as a people—as a human race—to help us remember that value is intrinsic, to help nurture the good parts of us that have been buried but have been exposed through this*

time when we have been hurt, forced into this vulnerable place, and fruit is born of vulnerability."

On Palm Sunday, King Jesus rides a humble donkey into Jerusalem towards his death. While unaware of the leaders' plot to arrest and kill Jesus, his followers shout, "Hosanna! Hosanna! Blessed is he who comes in the name of the Lord!" At churches on Palm Sunday the liturgy comes to life as children wave palm branches, shout Hosanna, and play the role of the unknowing followers, less than one week before Christ's betrayal and crucifixion. Jesus heading into Jerusalem on a donkey is Jesus moving into the very heart of human vulnerability: the cross. At the crossroads of suffering and abandonment Jesus hung there more or less naked, and *fruit was born of vulnerability.*

Jesus' humility to ride on a donkey into his own vulnerability tells us something about our God. God's power is revealed in humility and vulnerability. God's strength is revealed in love and justice. The fruits of salvation, born of Jesus' vulnerability as he hung on the tree and died for you and me, were forgiveness, community, sacrifice, and love. In vulnerable moments—births, deaths, grief, global pandemics, first dates, break-ups, last days in a place or a job you love—pay attention, and allow yourself to be vulnerable, for *fruit is born of vulnerability.*

Question

As we prepare for Jesus' death in Holy Week, have you thought about preparing for your own death? Have you and your family talked with one another about your wishes for your body when you die? While this may seem awkward and it is indeed vulnerable, it can turn out to be a meaningful conversation to have with those you love. The 5 Wishes (5wishes.org) is a wonderful resource we recommend.[13]

Prayer

Hosanna! Hosanna!
Sweet King Jesus,
We praise You and yet we feel the tension
as we look down the road of this Holy Week
and see the stark darkness to come on Good Friday
which was not *good, but rather violent.*
Caught in the tension, we pray for perspective, O God.
We know that this same kind of tension exists in our daily lives
where joy and fear, hopes and grave disappointments,
marriage and betrayal, love and hate, life and death
all intermingle.
Help us, we pray, when conflicts in life appear black and white,
to see a third, perhaps more holy, more colorful way,
and to navigate through the confusing waters of this wild world.
Humble us, completely, through the mysterious hours of this holy week.
Prepare our minds and hearts to receive the miracle of Easter Sunday
by accompanying us through this sacred story.

---

[13] Please note that this may involve a legal document in certain states.

163

Thank you that your love for humanity
is greater than any height, or width, or depth we can
imagine.
We pray these things in Sweet King Jesus' name.
Amen.

VII

The Arrested, Executed and Resurrected One

Holy Week

41

Monday: Ode to Extravagant Feelers

"Mary took a pound of costly perfume made of pure nard, anointed Jesus' feet, and wiped them with her hair. The house was filled with the fragrance of the perfume."
   - John 12:3

Acrylic painting by Anonymous

Reflection

As a child, I got the sense that my feelings were something that needed to be fixed. My expression of feelings was labeled as "dramatic" or "too much." My feelings were symptoms that needed to be treated. To this day, shame still lingers in the shadows every time I show my true self to the world, every time that deeply feeling child emerges, who knew the contours of every sadness, joy, and fear. The aftertaste of shame tries to convince me that others will soon reject me. It is the fear of being labeled "too much," and being left "not enough."

But doesn't Jesus accept extravagant feelings? Mary exceeded extravagance. Mary expended a pound of perfume valued at about the yearly income of a manual laborer, and used her hair to wipe it on Jesus' feet.

I imagine Jesus looking at me as a child, that child who lived out loud and defied what was "normal," who would've wiped Jesus' feet with her hair, covered in perfume, in a lavish display of love and gratitude. I imagine Jesus looking at me with a face full of love and compassion. Jesus didn't reject Mary, so why would he reject me? Jesus is on the side of the feelers, the ones deemed "too much," the ones who make us uncomfortable with their displays of emotion. I pray that child still exists, somewhere inside of me. I pray that society's expectations of how I should act and who I should be wouldn't keep me from falling at Jesus' feet.

-Pastor Riley

Prayer

Lord, help us to feel.
Let us be moved by our gratitude and love to worship you.
You alone are worthy of our praise.
Thank you, Lord.
Thank you for loving us lavishly
and for accepting in return our lavish acts of love.
Amen.

42

Tuesday: God Chose What Is Foolish

*"For God's foolishness is wiser than human wisdom,
and God's weakness is stronger than human strength.
Consider your own call, brothers and sisters: not many
of you were wise by human standards, not many were
powerful, not many were of noble birth. But God chose
what is foolish in the world to shame the wise; God chose
what is weak in the world to shame the strong; God chose
what is low and despised in the world, things that are not,
to reduce to nothing things that are, so that no one might
boast in the presence of God."*
  - 1 Corinthians 1:25-29

Litany

God chose what is foolish in the world
  Why do we love to remember Jesus as a wise teacher,
  but forget that he came into the world as a helpless baby
  and told a rich man to give away everything he owned?

God chose what is weak in the world

Why do we love to remember how Jesus performed miracles and healed people,

yet we gloss over his anger in the temple

and his weeping over a dear friend who died?

God chose what is low and despised in the world

Why do we love to remember Jesus as King,

but get uncomfortable remembering

that Jesus was also homeless, a refugee, and a prisoner?

The message of the cross is foolishness to those who are perishing,

but to those who are being saved it is the power of God.

Question

In what ways do "wisdom" and "foolishness" play out for us today? Where does power and social capital lie? Are we truly willing to forfeit our standing in the status quo in order to live according to Christ's way?

Prayer

> *Almighty God,*
> *I want to feel strong. Help make me strong.*
> *Not strong like war; strong like peace. Strong-souled.*
> *Make me strong enough to love my enemies*
> *and strong enough to forgive others and myself.*
> *Help me to be strong enough to follow the path of discipleship*

and strong enough to leave judgment to God.
King Jesus, who rode a humble donkey,
help me to be strong enough to be kind,
to share, to cry, to laugh,
strong enough to nurture and to lead and to follow You.
Make me strong-hearted, Lord,
strong like peace.
All powerful, all loving Lord,
my strength is in You, my Rock and my Redeemer.
Amen.

43

Wednesday: Judas' Humanity, Our Humanity

"After saying this Jesus was troubled in spirit, and declared, 'Very truly, I tell you, one of you will betray me.' The disciples looked at one another, uncertain of whom he was speaking."

- John 13:21-22

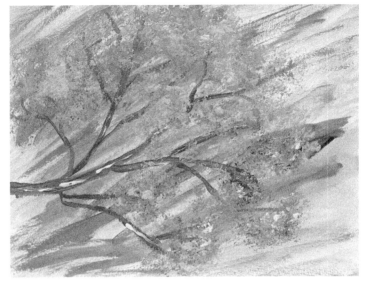

"Judas' Tree," acrylic painting by Anonymous

Reflection

There are two aspects to this scene in John 13: Jesus foretelling his betrayal, and how the disciples respond to it.

Jesus knew he was going to be betrayed by one of his disciples and he knew that betrayal would lead to his death, yet he sat in it. He didn't pass judgment or try to stop it. He let it trouble him. He also let it unfold.

It's a stark contrast with the disciples' first instinct to look around at *everyone else* besides themselves. This reveals something profound about our humanity and our inclination toward self-preservation. It seems hardwired into our nature to look outward before we look inward. I wonder what would change if our first instinct was to look inward and recognize

174

our own capacity to betray and hurt the ones we love before we so quickly look outward and point the finger? I wonder what would change if we put more energy into comforting those who are betrayed rather than focusing so much energy on blame and figuring out "who done it"?

In a sense, history has not let Jesus' betrayer, Judas, be fully human. We define him by his mistake and therefore distance ourselves from him. We haven't acknowledged how we too might have made the same choice. We haven't acknowledged how he too was fully human.

Prayer

> *Holy God,*
>   *Help us to not be so quick to turn, blame, and point the finger,*
>   *but rather help sit in the discomfort of self-reflection.*
>   *Give us the courage to turn inward*
>   *and the awareness to resist the tendency to point fingers.*
>   *Help us to avoid scapegoating*
>   *and instead recognize that we all hold a capacity for great love*
>   *and for great harm.*
>   *Guide us toward love.*
>   *Amen.*

44

Maundy Thursday: Shouldn't Jesus Be Painted on a Throne?

"Jesus, knowing that the Father had given all things into his hands, and that he had come from God and was going to God, got up from the table, took off his outer robe, and tied a towel around himself. Then he poured water into a basin and began to wash the disciples' feet and to wipe them with the towel that was tied around him."

- John 13:3-5

Revolutionary Love by C.

Jesus, Misunderstood Jesus
They arrested you and hung you on a tree
For loving all those poor people as hard as I've ever seen
Your forgiveness of sinners, your acceptance and your grace
The Empire became threatened by the mere presence

of your face

O, Jesus, Revolutionary Jesus
   Speaking parables so potent you made the unjust power structures tremble
   Planting seeds of mercy and resistance in the hearts and minds of those at the margins
   Empowering people with dignity and worth by telling them the truth
   God's mercy is for everyone—it doesn't cost a thing—just your life.
   All are welcome—just bring your heart and we'll start a revolution of love.

Reflection

I once had a conversation with someone who didn't consider themselves specifically Christian or religious in any way. I had commissioned him to do some artwork for a community garden church plant, and I asked him if he was familiar with Davinci's painting of the Last Supper. As an artist, he said he was. Then I started talking about how the team would really love it if he would paint Jesus washing the disciples' feet.

He was very thrown off, almost to the point of being offended. Except that he wasn't religious at all, so he had nothing to take offense at. He slowly gathered himself then said, "Shouldn't Jesus be painted up high on a throne? Or should he at least be in the center of the table or something? Why would he be washing people's feet?" It was such a good, simple, and reasonable question, and I was grateful to have the opportunity to get to tell the story of why Jesus—my sweet

Jesus—washed his disciples' feet the night he was betrayed and arrested.

-Crawford

Prayer

> *Gracious God,*
> *Help us to be more like you,*
> *a servant and a friend.*
> *Help us to be less concerned with status or hierarchy*
> *and more concerned with offering love and grace to all*
> *we encounter.*
> *Amen.*

45

Good Friday: Looking for Christ in the World

"So the soldiers, their officer, and the Jewish police arrested Jesus and bound him ...

They cried out, 'Away with him! Away with him! Crucify him!' Pilate asked them, 'Shall I crucify your King?' The chief priests answered, 'We have no king but the emperor.' ...

When Jesus had received the wine, he said, 'It is finished.' Then he bowed his head and gave up his spirit."

- John 18:12; 19:15; 19:30

Life Arrested by Rachel

In my eyes there is fear
In my heart there is hate
In my mind there is fury
In my life there is shame
These gates control me
These walls they haunt me
These chains that break me
This life that has changed me
My eyes full of tears with
No reason to fear
My heart it aches
There is so much to take
My mind it wanders

180

So full of rage
My life so crowded
Of those that blame
This prison is cold
The walls untold
These chains are short
My life is at court
My eyes they cry
My heart it aches
My mind it's angry
My life it blames me

Reflection

On this day, Jesus, our Lord and Savior, was betrayed and denied by his closest friends and companions. A group of people with torches and ill intentions found him in the middle of the night and took him to multiple dignitaries hoping to end his life. He was beaten by police. He was arrested and judged guilty. He was proclaimed to be a sinner and a blasphemer. He was incarcerated. A mob of people made it known that they would not be satisfied until he was dead. He was flogged and tortured. He was laughed at by crowds of people. He was isolated and alone. He was executed by the Roman State, publicly shamed for his life's work. He was stripped naked for the thrill of playing a game. After he died, his body was removed quickly as to not be an undignified reminder of his torture during the holy worship of Passover.

It is clear in the Passion narrative that when God became human, God slipped into "the vulnerability of skin and entered a world as violent and disturbing as our own."[14] In any way we suffer, Christ whispers in the passion narrative, "I suffer alongside of you in this." The part of this story that makes us uncomfortable is also the birthplace of hope because it is the clue to how we find God in our world and it is where we find our calling as Christ's servants. The sadness, suffering, and death, the incarceration, the beatings, the humiliation, and the mistreatment are vital parts of the story that bear witness to the truth that God has come to the worst places and the most painful circumstances and, by the power of the Holy Spirit, God shares in our suffering. God is there with us in the midst of tragedy to bear our burdens and our sorrows.

Good Friday illuminates where we find God in our world. Today, people around the globe are suffering in the very ways that Jesus did 2,000 years ago. We must lift up our eyes and wonder: what in our world breaks God's heart? Who in our world is being sought out in the middle of night with metaphorical torches and real ill intentions? Who is beaten by police? Who is arrested and condemned? Who are the incarcerated? Who is sought out by mobs and condemned to die? Who is mocked? Who are the isolated and alone? Who are the undignified that we try to avoid when we come to worship?

These questions, though they might make us uncomfortable, will allow the Holy Spirit to illuminate where Christ is in our world. The whisper running throughout the Gospel of John's Passion narrative is that when we are looking for Jesus in our world we shouldn't look to the noble or regarded or beautiful, but rather to those who suffer like Christ. It is amongst the

---

[14] Nadia Bolz Weber, *Accidental Saints: Finding God in the Wrong People*, (New York: Convergent Books, 2015).

suffering people of the world that we will find the Presence of Christ.[15]

Prayer

> *Executed God, Crucified Christ,*
>   *Open our eyes to You in this world.*
>   *Point us to the ones who are suffering today like you suffered.*
>   *Fill us with compassion so that we might come alongside them,*
>   *that we might get close and really see them.*
>   *Make us uncomfortable so that we can more clearly see your Spirit at work*
>   *and be moved to participate in Your work here on Earth.*
>   *Amen.*

---

[15] Excerpt from a sermon given by Pastor Layne entitled *Looking for God in All the Wrong Places* on April 19, 2019 at St. Leo's Catholic Church in Tacoma, WA.

46

Holy Saturday: Sitting Vigil

*"So Joseph took the body and wrapped it in a clean linen
cloth and laid it in his own new tomb, which he had hewn
in the rock. He then rolled a great stone to the door of the
tomb and went away. Mary Magdalene and the other
Mary were there, sitting opposite the tomb."*
    - Matthew 27:59-61

No Hope In View by C.B.

Eyes cast down—Jesus in the ground
   Music has ceased—praying for release
   All direction lost—and he died at what cost?
   Those two thieves by his side—Jesus' justice denied
   Barabbas runs loose—and not a thing I can do
   The tears just keep coming—is it time to start running?
   Just last week we waved palms ... and today ... he is
gone.
      Tomorrow I'll grieve at the garden and pray—these

tears have become too much for today.

To picture him there wrapped up in linen is an unbearable end so I'll hold fast to the beginning—that day that Jesus called me by name ... and from that day on life would never be the same.

The greatest miracle I ever saw was a simple act of love—a human interaction with God up above.

Jesus was coming to town, and there was a man in a tree—a tax collector he turned out to be.

Jesus called him down and invited him to dinner, and right then and there, Zaccheus repented as a sinner.

Jesus always loved the outcast, the lonely and the sick—ever since I knew him. You could say they were what made him tick?

But it was something else too—for I believe he's God's only Son—I just can't believe he died ... I can't believe death won.

O Jesus, my sweet Jesus, what have they done to you? Darkness falls, confusion reigns—I can see no hope in view.

Excerpt from *The Mystery of Death* by Dorothy Soelle

"In most cultures the care of and companionship to the dying, as well as the washing and anointing of the dying, are matters belonging to women, as are the rituals of weeping and lamenting the dead. Jesus is quite aware of this. While his disciples consider it absurdly wasteful when a woman anoints him in Bethany, Jesus sees it as a preparation for his death (Matt. 26:12). The women

seem to live closer to death than the dominant sex."[16]

Reflection

The Matthew 27 text in the lectionary today describes Joseph preparing Jesus' body, wrapping it in fresh linen, lying it in the tomb, rolling the stone in front of the door of the tomb, and leaving. Joseph's grief and pain take him away from the body. No judgment. That's just the way the story goes.

At the same time, we read that Mary Magdalene and "the other Mary" were there too, and as Matthew tells it, they chose to sit there opposite the tomb. Who knows how long they sat there. They sat there in their grief. No judgment. Because there is no right way to grieve.

Let me say that again for the people in the back row: THERE IS NO RIGHT WAY TO GRIEVE!

I am brought back to a time when I was in my own valley of the shadow of death. I was sick and scared, not able to get out of bed. A housemate I had at the time saw me in my disorientation and pain and sat on the ground with her back right up against my bed for hours in silence, holding the space for me. She sat vigil.

Several years ago, Pastor Layne's grandmother passed away from complications following a stroke. She received a phone call from her mother early one morning who called to let her know that her grandmother was being admitted to hospice care and would not be with them much longer. She quickly made arrangements with work and coordinated travel, but she

---

[16] Dorothy Soelle, *The Mystery of Death*, (Minneapolis: Fortress Press, 2007), pp. 53-54.

wasn't the only one.

Cousins, uncles, and aunts all drove or flew in, and the very next day everyone was there alongside Layne, gathered around her grandma's bedside. They sat vigil for the next two days. They took turns holding her hand, soothing her anxiety, reading scripture aloud, and giving her pain medication as prescribed. They gathered as a group and sang her favorite songs and told their favorite family memories. They got up close and sat in the holy pain of goodbye.

The two Marys sat vigil, too. They sat across from the tomb as Jesus descended into hell, as our God suffered. They got right up close to death and held space for lament and weeping. Little did they know that this ritual—this liminal space of waiting and weeping—was vital and necessary for what came next.

-Pastor Riley

Prayer

God,

Sometimes this in-between space feels like hell on Earth.

Sometimes justice delayed feels like justice denied.

Sometimes it feels like your absence,

and stories of resurrection and new life sound like a fairy tale.

In this in-between space,

where it feels like we're straddling life and death,

wrestling with doubt and clinging to faith,

we acknowledge we are completely lost without you, God.

187

We are here in the Saturday silence,
amidst the darkness of doubt,
and as your people we wait still
with great expectation for the coming dawn.
May this prayer be a cue to prepare our hearts for a
resurrection and a rebirth
as we wait in the darkness, in the silence, in the stillness
of the midnight hour,
as we wait and know that You are God.
Amen.

47

Easter: Resurrection of the Lord

"Jesus said to her, 'Woman, why are you weeping? Whom are you looking for?' Supposing him to be the gardener, she said to him, 'Sir, if you have carried him away, tell me where you have laid him, and I will take him away.' Jesus said to her, 'Mary!' She turned and said to him in Hebrew, 'Rabbouni!' (which means Teacher) ... Mary Magdalene went and announced to the disciples, 'I have seen the Lord'; and she told them that he had said these things to her."

- John 20:15-16; 18

"Untitled," watercolor by Anonymous

Unchained Melody by Rachel

These walls all combined
   Our feelings all entwined
   Gates cutting into our hate
   Police colliding, taking our pride
   Controlling the pace
   Without the space
   Outside is high, the sky is free
   Angels are protecting our cries
   Glorious God, the Almighty King
   Hears our calls, such melodies
   Broken hearts, breaking chains

190

Deliver us from these gates
This prison is a time to change
It's time to relinquish the pain
Our space is confined
But our hope is much stronger
This time behind razor wire
Is our chance to be new

Reflection

In this text there is so much good news, but also there is also so much not-recognizing-the-good-news. After all, the good news is coming from unexpected people. First, Mary accuses Jesus of hiding the body because she does not recognize Jesus, and then the disciples do not trust that Mary saw Jesus.

I wonder how many times we might miss out on good news because we are not listening to the person who is sharing it? Maybe we are too busy with our lives to take notice of the stranger we pass. Maybe we walk right past Jesus while simultaneously wondering why Jesus isn't answering our prayers. Maybe someone is telling us the good news we need, but because they do not meet whatever standard we think a preacher or a Christian or a [fill in the blank] should meet, we don't listen to what they have to say.

As the pastor of a prison congregation, it is clear to me that although the incarcerated have good news to share with the world, it is often overlooked, locked up, and kept at a distance. Because we have allowed fear and distance to define our relationship to those who are incarcerated, we are missing out on a profound gospel that the world deeply needs. It is my experience that too many bright and talented individuals are ending up in prison and we as a society need to find ways to do better to connect, reconnect, and stay connected to one another. I wonder who in your life might have news to share that could change your life? How might you learn from the Easter story to listen more openly and see more clearly?

-Pastor Layne

Prayer

Living Christ,
Thank you for coming down and dwelling among us,
for teaching us, walking with us, healing us,
Suffering with us, dying for us,
and rising from the grave to show us
that love always has the final word.
Send your Holy Spirit among us this day,
giving us resurrection ears and resurrection eyes
so that we might experience your good news
in unexpected places and from unexpected people.
Amen.

About the Artists

Hagar's Community Church is a congregation of the Olympia Presbytery, a sanctuary for God's beloved exiles on the inside of the Washington Corrections Center for Women. Their mission is to give incarcerated individuals their own Christian community through which they might explore their spirituality and encounter the proclamation and experience of God's love.

Why Hagar?

Hagar's Story is found in Genesis 16 and 21. She is a woman to whom history has been unkind, much like the women who are incarcerated at the WCCW. Hagar is often seen as "the other woman," a woman who was mean to Sarah, a foreigner, slave, the unknown. Hagar is not someone lifted up as a hero of our faith. When you read her story, however, it becomes apparent that though history is unkind, God is not. Rather, God finds Hagar in the wilderness and blesses her with the same blessing that God gives Abraham- that she will be the mother of a nation. God provides for her and cares for her. Hagar is the first person in scripture to name God: "She gave this name to the Lord who spoke to her: 'You are the God who sees me,' for she said, 'I have now seen the One who sees me.'"(Genesis 16:13) There are many points of connection of Hagar's story to the women at the WCCW. When choosing this name, the women stated that they found it healing to know God is the One who sees them- and that they are indeed blessed.

Why Community?

The goal is to create fellowship and understanding among all who are part of our worshiping community. To cultivate trust and understanding in the midst of an environment where that is not often found. This is not just a worship service being offered where the women come to sit and hear a sermon and return back to their living unit. Rather we are creating an atmosphere of trust and belonging across all sorts of boundaries that exist at the WCCW. Our goal is to create true Christian fellowship that will nurture and sustain these women in the most trying of circumstances.

Why Church?

We are striving to create our own distinctive church that allows the women of the WCCW to belong and empowers them to make decisions about who we will be as congregation. It is a long term goal for this congregation to charter and be counted as its own distinctive congregation in the Olympia Presbytery. It is also our goal to hold space each week for the women of the WCCW to commune with and worship God.

You can find out more about Hagar's Community Church at hagarscommunitychurch.com.

Made in the USA
Coppell, TX
10 February 2021

50137945R10118